T0129178

Zen

and the Art of
Crossword
Puzzles

A Journey Down and Across

Nikki Katz

Adams Media
New York London Toronto Sydney New Delhi

Adams Media
An Imprint of Simon & Schuster, Inc.
57 Littlefield Street
Avon, Massachusetts 02322

For information about special discounts for bulk purchases, please contact Simon &
Schuster Special Sales at 1-866-506-1949 or business@simonandschuster.com.

The Simon & Schuster Speakers Bureau can bring authors to your live event. For
more information or to book an event contact the Simon & Schuster Speakers Bureau
at 1-866-248-3049 or visit our website at www.simonspeakers.com.

Manufactured in the United States of America

Library of Congress Cataloging-in-Publication Data
Katz, Nikki.
  Zen and the art of crossword puzzles / by Nikki Katz.
      p. cm.
  Includes index.
  ISBN 1-59337-563-8
1. Crossword puzzles. I. Title.

  GV1507.C7K38 2006
  793.73'2--dc22

                                    2006005210

ISBN 978-1-59337-563-8

Contents

To my husband, Jason, for your endless support
and encouragement

Acknowledgments

This book is a culmination of education, humility, and openness—all on my part. I learned much more about Zen and crosswords than I ever thought possible, and I have my agent, Barb Doyen, and editor, Kate Epstein, to thank for this experience and opportunity. I also need to thank those people who were patient and expressive enough to speak with me about their favorite hobby and artistic outlets. I was blessed to have such a varied and vocal group of crossword fans willing to open their hearts, and I hope I articulated their thoughts and processes effectively.

Of course I could never have completed this work without the support of all my friends and family. You know who you are, and I hope you know how much I cherish everything you've done.

Introduction

When Zen practice is completely developed, there is no center, no extremes; there are no edges or corners. It is perfectly round and frictionless.

—Zen Master Hongzhi

I'd wager a guess that you don't solve crossword puzzles while meditating in the lotus position in a candlelit room, the scent of vanilla filling your nostrils as incense burns in the corner, pillows strewn all around, and your eyes closed lightly as you take deep breaths and meditate. It might be nice if you did—but a bit disruptive as you would have to take sneak peeks at the grid and clues before going back to your deep breaths. Instead of calm peaceful thoughts, your mind would race frantically to come up with the perfect solution.

This classic scene of meditation doesn't exactly meld well with solving crosswords, but there are several similar aspects and experiences that relate to both completing crossword puzzles and Zen. You can easily find yourself in a Zen-like state as you spend concentrated time focused on solving a puzzle. The world around you fades to the background as your mind works in harmony with your tool of choice. And even though you may not realize it, you often incorporate Zen philosophy and teachings when working through a crossword puzzle.

The word Zen derives from the Chinese word *Ch'an*, a major school of Buddhism which itself was derived from the Sanskrit word *dhyana*, meaning meditation. Zen is based on the belief that enlightenment can be attained through meditation, self-reflection, and intuition—placing minimal emphases on faith and devotion. Zen is a Buddhist tradition that originated in India before it traveled to China and then Japan. Buddhism began approximately 2,500 years ago when Siddhartha Gautama, a prince of the area that is now India, meditated under The Bodhi Tree and achieved awakening. Then known as Buddha, he wandered for many years teaching his views—that life is permeated with suffering caused by desire, that suffering ceases when desire ceases, and that enlightenment obtained through right conduct, wisdom, and meditation releases one from desire and suffering.

According to Robert Allen in his book *Zen Questions*, anyone can practice Zen. "Zen sees itself as only one of many paths to liberation. It does not, therefore, reject other people's beliefs." Zen is a path of exploration, not a religion. People from all spiritual beliefs and walks of life are welcome to attempt the journey and are encouraged to do so. Zen is about the experience of enlightenment, not the rules for achieving it or the ideas that describe it. Anyone can believe in Zen; few realize its enlightenment.

Core beliefs of Zen are that all things are connected, everything is in harmony, and everything is fluid and changing. We are one with each other, the animals, and the Earth. The only boundaries that exist are the false ones we create in our minds. In Zen, it is crucial to break those notions and rid ourselves of any attachments to our ego, or false notion of self. Suffering occurs when we hold on to something that is not ours. This includes material objects, as well as the people and relationships that we work to protect and hold tight in our lives. In being connected with everything around us, there is no need to grasp and own. In having nothing, you have everything.

Zen in itself is not a tool that will help you be a better crossword puzzle solver, although some of the Zen philosophies work to assist you in accepting mistakes and digging into your subconscious to find hidden solutions. Mainly the Zen teachings will influence you and help you to master your inner self. You may find yourself using calming techniques and clearing your thoughts before starting to solve a puzzle—moving yourself into a working meditation as you find the rhythm of the crossword puzzle and the minutes tick by without any care. This is similar to the trance people feel when they are enthralled in their task, one that completely takes over and allows them to be at harmony with the world.

When Zen blends with art, it culminates in a weave of humanity and its surroundings. Art is the human effort to imitate and supplement nature. It is about expressing yourself, observing the world around you, and being skilled in performing tasks. In his book *Zen and the Art of Making a Living*, Laurence G. Boldt wrote, "You can experience your everyday life as art by bringing to it the qualities of the artist—inspiration and absorption, creativity and resourcefulness, play and delight." Indeed crossword-puzzle solving incorporates all of these traits and allows the puzzle solver to embody the qualities of the artist. When I solve a crossword puzzle, I use it as a diversion and playtime. I am forced to use creativity and my own resourcefulness to solve the tougher clues. I am most definitely absorbed in the crossword—at least if I am intent on finishing the puzzle—and can find inspiration in the themes or clues given. And then there is the art of crossword puzzles themselves. The crossword mania that has swept the world since 1913 has resulted in a variety of artistic impressions, including books, paintings, advertisements, and vanity license plates—to name a few.

Zen and the Art of Crossword Puzzles serves to explore crossword puzzles through a potpourri of personal narratives, interviews, quotes, and news articles on the techniques and tools for solving puzzles, using puzzles to guide and assist you in life, constructing puzzles, and more. In my quest for interview subjects, I found many people willing to give their thoughts on their beloved hobby—a judge, a teacher, a mother, a fiancé, a software analyst, a retiree, and others from a variety of aspects of life. I spoke to people in Australia, England, and everywhere in between. Throughout the following chapters and stories, you'll find a gentle weaving of Zen philosophies and the ways they often parallel the construction and solving of crossword puzzles.

Chapter One

You Have to Start Somewhere

Take the first step, and your mind will mobilize
all its forces to your aid. But the first essential is that you begin.
Once the battle is startled, all that is within and without
you will come to your assistance.

— Robert Collier

Can you remember the first time you picked up a crossword puzzle, set your mind to work on the clues, and carefully wrote in the answers with a pen, or pencil? Perhaps a favorite teacher introduced you to the activity when you were young, or you picked it up on your own one day as you sat in the waiting room waiting to see your doctor for your annual checkup. And now, as your love of solving has grown and expanded, do you find that your methods have changed? Maybe now you solve everything in pen, to prove to yourself that you aren't afraid of mistakes. And perhaps now you sit down daily with a crossword in your favorite position at the dining-room table after dessert each evening. Whatever the circumstances, whatever the traditions that got you here today, with this book, you began with a crossword. That first step has been taken by millions of fans across the globe, and it gives you a commonality you may have never perceived to exist. This chapter will introduce the histories and methodologies of various solvers, including myself. I'll also discuss the pen-versus-pencil debate and the interesting process of picking up the pieces of an unknown solver's crossword attempt.

A Brief History

The crossword puzzle was created in December 1913 by Arthur Wynne of Liverpool, England. It was a diamond-shaped puzzle, published in the "Fun" section of the Sunday edition of the *New York World*. The game was titled a "word-cross" (it later was renamed a "cross-word" and the hyphen was eventually dropped) and immediately attracted a huge following. Within ten years, many American newspapers were including their own weekly puzzles.

Outside of the United States, other countries began introducing crossword puzzles after the conclusion of World War I. The first British crossword puzzle was printed in February 1922 in *Pearson's Magazine*. British puzzles quickly developed their own style, far more cryptic and difficult than American puzzles. The *New York Times* was one of the last newspapers to join the crossword craze, which is surprising considering the familiarity now associated with their puzzles. The *Times* began its weekly puzzle in 1942.

Simon & Schuster released the first book of crossword puzzles in the early 1920s. The small publishing house found instant success, selling about a quarter million copies of the book within the first year of publication. People began wearing crossword-themed clothing, and songs and stage shows involving crossword puzzles made their way onto the scene. Crosswords had made a grand entrance and were here to stay.

Some people believe the crossword puzzle to be a distant relative to word squares, a popular puzzle for the children of nineteenth century England. The technique behind the word square was established in ancient times—one from the first century was even found in the ruins of Pompeii. A word square is constructed by taking a word (of any length, although the shorter the word, the easier the square is to complete) and writing that same word in a grid—across and down. The square is then filled in with other words, such that each word can also be read both across and down, in the same positions (i.e. second down and second from the left). Here's an example:

SHORE
HONOR
ONION
ROOMS
ERNST

The largest legitimate word squares are constructed using words nine letters in length, although people continue to attempt to create ten-letter squares—many using computers in their quest.

The Beginning of a Memory

My personal crossword history isn't a lengthy one. Approximately eight years ago, before my husband and I had children, a business to run, pressing engagements, and a to-do list that stretched out end-lessly, we solved crossword puzzles together. This was the first time in my life that I did crosswords regularly. Back then, our weekends were free and empty. We tried out a variety of activities, some that would eventually help define our relationship. One of our favorites was spending a quiet evening together solving a crossword puzzle. On a typical Friday evening, we left our small condominium in La Jolla, California, and headed to the local supermarket to pick up a copy of the *National Enquirer*. We strolled hand in hand, or drove in those rare instances of rain or cold weather, to a nearby coffee shop with our magazine and pencil.

We stood in line with other young couples just starting off their evenings and ordered hot drinks and a decadent dessert. We walked to the back of the room to sprawl on a couch or two chairs with a table, taking a moment to stare at the ocean waves crashing below us, illuminated by lights from nearby restaurants. After a few sips of a latte and a couple of bites of carrot cake, I'd open the magazine and turn straight to the crossword puzzle. We particularly enjoyed solving the *National Enquirer* puzzles because they were color-coded—the consonants clearly discern-able from the vowels. Some people may consider this cheating, but I consider it a five-second head start on the game.

My husband and I have different methods for starting cross-word puzzles, but they mesh together nicely. I begin by silently reading the clues down the page and writing in any solutions I know. My husband starts by visually skipping around the clues, looking for anything obvious that jumps out at him. One of us is the pencil holder, who enters in the crossword answers as they are solved, regardless of who comes up with the solution. I typically hold that task, as I have the better handwriting.

As the evening progressed and we continued solving clues, there was an easy lob back and forth as if we played a leisurely game of tennis. I'd scribble down an answer, giving my husband an extra letter in the line he was working on, and he'd solve another entry. We continued this way until the page was full, our brains were satiated, our coffee mugs were empty, and the last bite of cake was licked clean from the fork. We were calm, relaxed, and very much in tune with one another.

The only way we completed those crossword puzzles, enjoying rich coffee and each other's company, was by starting somewhere. If we hadn't answered a clue, we would have been left staring at a page full of text and some grids. By starting those puzzles, we learned to work together. We learned that different styles of solving a puzzle aren't necessarily a bad thing, which is great considering we have different styles when it comes to a lot of situations.

I am the type of person who deals with issues head-on, especially when it involves our relationship. My husband likes to procrastinate, and he will often push off a serious discussion for another time and place. Through those evenings solving crossword puzzles, I discovered that his mind works in a different way from mine. I methodically work through scenarios to find a solution to our challenges. He is able to play with ideas for a while, mull a solution over in his head, and then discuss it when the time is right for both of us. His approach used to infuriate me, as I wanted to work on an answer right when a problem occurred. He preferred to ignore me and would typically head off to sleep. Over the years, we've reached a happy medium. He will work with me when I really do need an immediate answer, and I know that in most instances, we can wait until a better time to find a solution.

As our relationship has grown and had its ups and downs, we've learned to mesh our methods together to find a place where we are both comfortable, at least most of the time. And I like to think that it all stems back to those Friday evenings solving crossword puzzles at the coffee house.

Settling In

There are many different ways and places that people solve crossword puzzles, each as unique and fitting as the puzzle itself. Whether you're curled up in bed with a book of crosswords, or sitting in a cafeteria with your turkey sandwich and chips half eaten at your side, the goal is to enjoy yourself and that moment to its fullest. Nowadays I tend to sit at my desk, one leg tucked under me in what my husband calls a "horrible posture" position, and type my way through a crossword online. If I don't complete it, I leave it open with a plethora of other windows that together render an image of my interests and projects.

Other people have their own ways to work through crosswords. Angela Thor, a librarian from Syracuse, New York, considers herself pretty lucky. "Our local newspaper has not one, but two crossword puzzles most days," she said. "We have a generic one Monday through Saturday, the Monday Monster, and the time-honored *New York Times* puzzle seven days a week. I started working the daily puzzle in the morning over breakfast."

The crossword puzzle was a way to keep morning, and her family to an extent, at bay until Angela was ready to face them. "The daily puzzle was about my speed, and I didn't have to look for too many answers. Then I tried the *New York Times*." That was all well and good for the first few days of the week, Angela said, but by the end, she was looking up more of the solutions than she was answering herself. This caused a slight change in the routine. "I started working on the puzzle a day late so that I always had the solution handy," she explained. "My daughter called it cheating. I called it improving my knowledge base, and there's nothing we librarians like more than cramming more information into our brains. I still don't do much of the Friday and Saturday *Times*, and haven't even attempted the Holy Grail: the Sunday *New York Times*."

Angela does her puzzles in pen—her officially designated crossword puzzle pen, which she explains has a good feel in her hand and writes smoothly. "Even though I keep reminding my kids to do their math in pencil, I still like doing the puzzle in ink, writing over mistakes without the least bit of guilt." When Angela doesn't have time to complete a puzzle, she cuts it out before recycling the paper. "I can tell when I'm in need of some 'me' time by how many puzzles are stacked up, so they act as a warning signal. Look out, Mom's got twenty undone puzzles, and she's going to blow."

There's something satisfying to Angela in knowing obscure bits of information, like Roman numerals beyond X. She loves the wink and nudge you get from some of the answers—figuring out the pun, finding the new way of looking at a clue. "Sometimes I can look at a clue in the morning and be, well, clueless," Angela said. "Then I'll look at it sometime later, and it's like, 'That's so simple.' Even working out the theme can be a challenge."

Angela noted that solving puzzles doesn't save the world, but it does help save her family from a crabby mom. It gives her a lift. As Helen Keller once wrote, "I long to accomplish a great and noble task, but it is my chief duty to accomplish small tasks as if they were great and noble." A crossword puzzle can make the doer smile and frown and scratch her head, and after she's done, she can look at the world around her with maybe a little different insight.

Coffee and Crosswords

Crosswords and coffee seem to make a good mixture for most people. Although it may make it too easy to eat your way through that last half of the apple pie you made for dessert while you're distracted, there's something perfect about settling down with a crossword for your brain to munch on and a hot drink, with or without a snack, to keep your mouth busy.

Claudia Tropila, an attorney from Huntington Beach, California, starts each and every morning with the *Los Angeles Times* crossword puzzle. "Between that and a couple of cups of coffee, I feel like I actually have kick-started my brain for the day," she said. "At home in the evening, I often pick up the British crypto puzzles I have downloaded from Dave T. [a moderator for *www .crossword.org*] or gotten from other places on the Web and fiddle around doing the best I can, sometimes with a gin and tonic, before I start preparing dinner." On weekends, puzzles are a source of relaxation. Claudia works most weekends at home, and she promises herself that she gets to solve a puzzle if she gets the job done. "I have to say that I am very good at American puzzles, including the diagramless [grids without any black squares or numbers] ones, and took up doing the British versions because I felt I wasn't being challenged enough," Claudia said. While Claudia can usually finish 99 percent of the U.S. puzzles she starts, she finds she can complete only about 5 percent of the U.K. ones, something that she finds very frustrating. But that certainly isn't going to stop her from trying.

Rosie Paquette, a small business owner/operator from Toronto, Canada, solves crosswords daily at her desk at home over breakfast and coffee and at her desk at work at noon while eating her lunch. She always uses the same kind of pen, "Paper Mate, medium point blue," and keeps dry white-out handy for potential mistakes. Her first preference for crossword puzzle sources is the newspaper. "I love the feeling of my favorite pen on the soft newspaper print," she said. On weekends, Rosie does the "Prize" puzzle in the *Toronto Star* over the telephone with a good friend. It usually takes them ninety minutes to complete the puzzle. "We chat and solve," she related. "It's a cherished Sunday tradition."

Keith Long, a singer and civil servant from Kingston upon Thames, Surrey, has three main locations for solving puzzles. The first is the sofa at his home, always at the right-hand end, near a table with a lamp, with pens, pencils, and a dictionary surrounding him. The second location is when he's on the train heading to work. It's "almost always the first thing I do when I get on the train, and I regard it as a disappointment if I don't complete the puzzle between the Kingston and Wimbledon stations," Keith said. The third locale is in the pub at lunchtime or after work.

"A proper ritual" is what Susanna Duffy, an adult education teacher and radio journalist from Melbourne, Australia, calls her methodology for solving a crossword. Without this exact process, Susanna feels that her hopes of completing the puzzle are doomed. "There are two types of crossword, one for the home and one for the train," she explained. "In the home, it's sufficient to settle in a favorite chair with a fountain pen and the crossword spread out any which way (first making sure the cat is comfortable). For the train, it must not be opened before taking your seat, it is neatly folded onto the left knee, and an answer written in fountain pen by each stop."

Pen Versus Pencil

Many people believe that the true skill of a crossword solver is evident looking at the utensil he uses to solve it with. The pencil typically indicates a beginner solver, one who is prone to making mistakes and needs the eraser handy to quickly clear away any errors in the grid. The pen symbolizes a sense of security and knowledge at the hands of the solver, as he knows if he makes a mistake he will be forced to mar the page to fix it. Of course these are just stereotypes and in multiple instances won't prove to be true. Many people just grab the first tool that is available, while others prefer the grip of a specific pencil or the familiar grasp of their favorite pen.

Personally, when I solve a crossword on paper, I use a pen. It's not necessarily because I believe that I won't make a mistake, but because I rarely have pencils in the house. And strange as it may sound, I do not own a pencil sharpener.

C.G. Rishikesh, a retired journalist from Chennai, India, told me that he used a pencil in the initial stages of his crossword-solving evolution, and then only sporadically. "The use of a pencil betrays a sense of tentativeness on the part of the solver," he said. "On the other hand, the use of pen exudes confidence and cocksureness. Besides, when the crossword is on newsprint, pencil makes faint impressions, and so even beginners may not prefer this writing instrument."

Pete Prindle explained, "People sometimes marvel at the fact that someone does a crossword puzzle in pen rather than pencil, but I maintain that the purpose of the exercise is to solve the puzzle in your mind, and then record that solution in the squares provided, rather than attack the problem with a trial-and-error approach." Peter's views probably result from his career as a Coast Guard rescue helicopter pilot—where you pretty much need to get it right the first time, or there may not be a second.

Taking the First Step

I can remember when my older daughter took her first step. She had been walking along furniture for well over a month, holding on to an object and steadying herself before moving her feet to carry her to another location. And then finally she decided to try walking without assistance. She stood up in the middle of our cream-colored carpet, looked around to determine her destination—my outstretched arms—and then did it. She lifted one chubby leg a centimeter off the floor and shakily placed it down on the floor in my direction. Gathering momentum, she lifted the other foot and toddled another step into my arms. Her self-esteem soared, and she was propelled forward into new activities and playground equipment she could now tackle.

Wouldn't it be great if every start ended in this manner—with people holding out their arms to offer support and opened doors for further exploration? That rarely happens, but that's not to say that we shouldn't initiate the starts in the first place. Once I take that first baby step in a project, I find that the task gets easier and more familiar. It's all about momentum. I see the work that I have accomplished behind me and that motivates me to move forward and extend myself further.

Starting crossword puzzles has helped to further my education and assuredness in taking those first steps. In writing down the answer to that first clue, I'm acknowledging that I will perform this task. I will see the puzzle through to the end. I am committing myself to the project. There are times that I just want to walk away:

I know that I won't have enough time to finish in one sitting, or the topic might be too difficult. Or maybe the design of the puzzle is beautiful as it is . . . without my handwriting and solutions to mar up the page. But once the first word is scrawled, I move on and don't look back. I do as much as I can and work toward the finish. My brain starts working, and I find that there is an increased momentum as I begin filling up the page. I become entrenched in the puzzle, allowing my mind to focus and strengthen, tuning out everything around me. There's no stopping me.

You Can't Finish if You Don't Start

There is a multitude of different ways to start a crossword puzzle—whether you are methodical and follow a discrete plan, or whether you start by scanning the clues to see if an answer materializes quickly. You have to determine what works for you and get your hand moving.

Just like puzzles, you can make new starts in your life via different paths. I know that when I start writing a new book, I sit down in front of the computer and type as fast as I can to get the words out of my head. I am always excited about a new idea and work feverishly until my mind is empty of thought. I then invariably find myself at a point where I'm done, but there isn't a complete novel on my desk. Sometimes there's not even a complete chapter. I have to backtrack, figure out what my goal is or what the plotline entails. I then have to write an outline and make sure that what I've previously written actually applies. But what is most important is that I moved forward and started the book.

When it comes to other tasks in my life, I find it easiest to get started if I have a detailed task list in spreadsheet form available. These help me get through any given project with as few headaches and missed deadlines as possible. The initial preparation is an integral part of how I start the job. Although this is a complete 180-degree switch from my method when it comes to writing, both ways of starting are ingrained in me, and I can execute them easily and successfully.

However I choose to start a project, it is important that I do it with a goal in sight. For most people, the goal of starting a crossword puzzle is to complete the task and have a grid full of correct answers. Depending on what else is going on, when I solve a puzzle, I may also have the goal of working my mind, having a good time, or enjoying an evening solving the puzzle with my family. The same applies to any other task in life. I set my goals and start the project, always keeping those goals in mind.

The First Time

The very first time you start a new activity or pick up a hobby can make or break whether you continue moving forward, learning and perfecting the craft. I remember the first time I went to the driving range to hit a golf ball. I picked up a club—this long, narrow, extension of my hand—and lifted it up. I swung down at that small white ball sitting about eight inches in front of my feet and watched as a big chunk of dirt and grass went flying out in front of me. I grabbed another ball from the large bucket to my right side, dropped it down, and then swung the club back over my head. This time I overcompensated and connected with nothing but air, almost throwing the club toward my friend who was standing next to me. Luckily I had brought along a comrade who knew what she was doing. She coached me on the proper hand grasp and where to place my feet in respect to the ball, depending on which club I was holding. She worked with me on my swing and my follow-through. Eventually I connected with the ball, only to watch it go diagonally across the grass, landing about twenty yards away. Not fabulous, but it was a start. Since that time, I've taken lessons, hit eighteen holes on small golf courses, and purchased my own set of clubs and a glove. That glove is essential for me to continue hitting anything more than ten balls on the driving range.

When it comes to crossword puzzles, I don't have a clear memory of starting them. I know that when I was growing up, my mom subscribed to *GAMES* magazine, and I would go through the various puzzles, solving where I could. As time progressed, I just instinctively knew what they were and how to solve them. There are other people who have wonderful stories of introductions to their crossword-solving futures, and perhaps someone even led them by the hand and taught them the ins and outs of the hobby.

Susanna Duffy said she learned how to solve crossword puzzles when she was six. "From my sixth birthday on, I spent every Sunday with my grandparents," she explained. "After lunch, I'd sit with my great-grandmother and go through the junior crossword. Over the next five years till her death, we tried every type of crossword imaginable, and I learned a lot about language skills from that old lady. We were thrilled when solving 'baroque' and 'grandiloquent,' and exulted with 'abstemious.' They were happy afternoons, happy days all round."

Terynon Powell, a pediatrician in the United Kingdom, helped his dad do crosswords in his teenage years and has dabbled at them ever since, often as a student with friends. "I really caught the bug in middle age when I tried the really difficult ones and found I could do them," he said pausing, "well, some of them." Terynon went on to say that he "was amazed by the variety and tricks the setters get up to in 'The Listener' crossword published weekly in the *Times*. I discovered that they keep statistics on your weekly entries, and that the real challenge was to go all year 'all correct,' achieved by very few. I've been trying ever since but have not found the Holy Grail yet!"

Richard Morse, a banker from Winchester, United Kingdom, first became interested in crossword puzzles because his father was an avid solver and had a good time with the answers he came up with. "We also played a lot of Scrabble as a family, which probably contributed, too," he said. Richard often solves crossword puzzles on trains or flights. On one such occasion, he was quietly solving "The Listener" crossword at a stopover in Sao Paulo from London to Santiago. The crossword was a mathematical one where there had been a typo corrected in a subsequent issue of the *Times*. "A sharp-eyed steward noticed me doing it and said that the Captain (who had left London before the emendation had been published) was feeling very frustrated at not being able to complete the crossword," Richard said. "I explained about the typo in a note sent up to the Captain. As a result, I was invited up to the flight deck for the rest of the flight, including a spectacular view of the Andes!" Richard went on to say, "The encouraging thing with a crossword is that you know it has a solution, unlike many problems in life where such a definite outcome is not assured."

Robert Wilde, a historian from Bedford, United Kingdom, said that about ten years ago he began solving a giant, thematic, crossword that was published on (or as near as publication allowed) Christmas Eve every year. "A decade later and the act of solving this puzzle on the night before Christmas is now as important to me as the turkey and presents of the next day."

Picking up the Pieces

Have you ever picked up a newspaper or magazine in a public location, only to find that the crossword puzzle has been worked halfway through? I worked as a management consultant for more than two years, and as part of my job I flew across the country weekly to various project sites. While on the airplane to and from my destination, I often worked on my laptop or curled up with my head against the window to catch up on my sleep. Other times I picked up the inflight magazine from my seatback pocket and browsed through the articles. At the back of the publication there was usually a crossword puzzle, and more often than not somebody had started to fill in the answers. Sometimes there appeared to be multiple people who had attempted the puzzle, indicated by the varying ink colors and styles of handwriting.

I saw this as a great challenge, trying to complete a puzzle that somebody else had started. I would take out my own writing utensil and lay the magazine on the seatback tray in front of me. I'd then go back through all of the clues to confirm that the answers that had been entered were indeed correct, or at the very least made sense if I didn't know the answers. I corrected any mistakes I saw, and then began to build off of the previous work. In some instances, the easy clues had all been answered, and I was left with the difficult ones. This forced me to immediately begin using all of my intellect rather than building on my puzzle-solving brain slowly as the crossword progressed. In other puzzles, the first solver had figured out the tough answers, leaving me with an easy and comfortable crossword session.

These crossword puzzles remind me a good deal of picking up the pieces of somebody else's assignment. As a consultant, I often came in to a company during the middle of a project and had to jump right in with the rest of the team. In these situations, I was left with an abundance of documents to read through. My goal was to understand the stage of the project, the members of the project team, the research that had been conducted, and the solutions that had been recommended. And just like the crossword puzzles, I would have to read back through the supporting documents and talk to the team members to determine if everything had been done correctly. If any mistakes had occurred, I had to fix them and then move forward with the plan. In some projects, the tough part had been completed, and I could soar through the rest of the task. In other assignments, the team had finished all of the easy work first, leaving me to attack the difficult tasks. In either case, I worked hard and finished the project to the best of my ability.

Try This

The next time you start a crossword puzzle, make a conscious effort to solve the clues in a different manner than you normally do. If you are a solver who reads through the clues and methodically answers each one, pick clues at random and see if the answers jump out at you. Or if you normally tackle a crossword puzzle haphazardly with no set plan, read through the clues in the order they are presented. Whatever new starts you implement, you may find that you don't catch as many answers the first time you begin. But you'll be teaching your brain a new way to attack fresh starts.

Much Ado about Crosswords

Ado
Ali
All
Asl
Bun
Cod
Cow
Del
Den
Eeg
Elm
Fen
Fig
Hoe
Ill
Lop
Mph
Nil
Nne
Odd
Pen
Sis
Sol
Spa
Uss
Wac

Aclu
Alky
Alpo
Clog
Coed
Duel
Dyer
Emir
Heir
Hobo
Hole
Idol
Loll
Long
Obie
Okra
Omit
Paso
Peer
Plat
Purl
Rued
Slip
Stop
Swab
Thai
Type
Word
Yell
Yogi

Adore
Aleph
Biped
Louis
Sales
Thyme

Across
Alegar

Adeptly
Boudoir

Complete
Lollygag

Chapter Two

Focus on the Important Pieces

If you understand, things are just as they are;
if you do not understand, things are just as they are.

—Zen proverb

Solving a crossword involves a cohesive recipe of knowledge and strategy with a pinch of insight and a good amount of luck. If you know which pieces to focus on, along with some tips of the trade, you're bound to find that edge that lets you get through those last few clues you couldn't previously decipher. It's also important to learn about being present and centered while solving puzzles, allowing those nagging peripheral thoughts to dissipate while you enjoy a moment of puzzle serenity.

Don't Be Clueless

The clues and the grid are the peanut butter and jelly of the crossword puzzle. Just as the sweet jelly makes the salty peanut butter taste better, the structured specifications of the grid make the freeform clues easier to unravel. The clues are your guidance and your assistance. The grid is your map and your navigation. Although they are not in the true essence of yin and yang, as they are not opposites of one another, the clues and grid follow the yin-yang model in that they are mutually dependent and cannot exist without the other. They are in balance (the same amount of clues as solutions in the grid), and they must interact with one another in a give and take. You need to use the clues and grid together to come up with a solution. When you see the clue "Hard headed," you may think up a variety of solutions, including NAIL, STUBBORN, STATUE, or one of a multitude of other words. But when you glance at the grid and see that there are squares for eight letters in the solution, you can quickly write the word STUB-BORN in those empty spaces. Without the grid, you'd be fumbling for the right answer. On the other hand, the grid would be nothing but white and black squares without the clues. You could fill it in with words, but they wouldn't necessarily be the puzzle solution that was intended.

There are two types of clues—straight and cryptic. Straight clues are the simpler of the two. These clues provide a definition, a fill in the blank, or a synonym to determine the answer, and they make up the majority of American crossword puzzles. Cryptic clues are much more involved. They use a variety of techniques to indirectly illustrate the meaning of the clue. Common methods include anagrams, container clues, charades, double definitions, homophones, reversals, hidden words, deletions, and any combination of the above. I discuss this further in Chapter 4.

Tricks of the Trade

You can have the calmness and security in Zen knowledge, but if you don't know how to solve a crossword correctly, you'll find yourself putting down the puzzle halfway through a sitting. You can't apply the principles of Zen until you have mastered the techniques and know-how to best work through a puzzle. Granted, if you're a Zen follower, your goal is not completion of the puzzle and perfection in the process, rather to have a good time and be present in the moment. But it doesn't hurt to have a few skills at your side.

If you're not quite a cruciverbalist expert (a cruciverbalist is a puzzle constructor or fan) you can better your techniques, and your time if you happen to test yourself against the clock, with some information and tips of the trade.

- If you're solving the *New York Times* crossword puzzle, Monday is the easiest day. The puzzles get progressively harder each day before culminating in the difficult Saturday edition. The Sunday puzzle is the largest of the week, but it has only a difficulty rating of a Thursday puzzle. When you're just starting off, work your way up through the days of the week, learn from your grid gaps, and soon you'll be completing with the best of them. You may be able to complete Monday and Tuesday puzzles for a few weeks before working your way completely through a Wednesday puzzle. You can always tackle a harder puzzle, but know your limitations and set your expectations accordingly.

■ Most people agree—don't insist on starting your solutions with 1 Across. If you know it, great, but if not, keep moving down the list of clues. It's best to scan through the clues and find ones you're pretty sure of. But don't write too soon. Don't jot down even one character until you are almost positive that the answer is correct. One way to double-check your answer is by crosschecking the perpendicular solutions. First memorize your potential answer, and then look at the intersecting clues for possible solutions to see if any of the letters match up. If you find one or two of the letters agree in each of your entries, feel free to enter in your solutions and move on.

■ Once you fill in a group of squares, focus on completing that section or quadrant until you've finished as much of the grid as possible. If you speak to crossword puzzle gurus, they refer to the quadrants in terms of their map coordinates. The NW part of the grid is the northwest, top left, area. SE is the bottom right, and so on. Look at the grid to determine the corresponding clues, rather than reading through the list of clues first. It is better to concentrate on one area of the grid at a time, that way you're not memorizing clues and cross-referencing answers all over the board. Work on a section until you feel you have exhausted your solutions, and then move on to another portion.

- The best place to start when you have a fresh grid is a clue that gives you a solution along the top row or left column, if you can figure out these clues. Why? Because those answers give you the first letters of any intersecting answers. Picture the grid in your mind. If you answer 1 Down, you are able to fill in the far left solution and give yourself the first letter of all of the corresponding perpendicular Across answers.

- Keep an open mind when it comes to the clues. Always remember that many English words have multiple definitions, so don't lock your mind around just one of them. If one definition doesn't result in a workable answer, move on to another usage. The worst possible clue in a crossword puzzle is the word set, as that word has 430 definitions in the *Oxford English Dictionary*. The word run takes a distant second place with 165 definitions.

- It helps to learn the rules of the clues. A question mark usually indicates something odd and is perhaps a cryptic clue or a pun. "Var." means that there is a variation of the spelling of the solution (usually slang such as NITE for NIGHT). If an abbreviation is used within the clue, or the clue is marked with the word (abbr.), you can bet that the answer will also be an abbreviation. This is also true if a foreign place is indicated in the clue; your solution will most likely be a word or phrase in the language of that location. You can also garner information to guess the ending letter of a solution. If the clue implies a plural answer ("Car movers") you can typically pen in an *s* as the last character of the solution (WHEELS). The same applies for an implied past-tense answer ("Consumed"), but in this case you'll write in *ed* as the final two characters (FIN-ISHED). Of course the answer could have been ATE, but by looking at the grid, you would know not to take up two of the three squares with the letters ED. Obviously all of these rules are subject to the puzzle and the constructor, and you'll need to use your best perception.

■ Lastly, allow your subconscious to work for you. Don't dawdle over a clue. If the answer is on the tip of your tongue, go ahead and spend a few more seconds on the solution. Otherwise you are better off moving on and letting your mind chew on the clue for a while. The longer you linger, the more time it will take to complete the puzzle. Although that may not matter to you in the beginning, as you progress in your crossword solving, you'll probably want to compete against the clock.

When you use all of these tips together, you have a powerful method for working through a crossword puzzle. Perhaps you knew them all, or only a few. Maybe you subconsciously follow these tools, and just now are able to put a voice to them. Taking it a step further, the act of learning about an activity before conducting it is a useful step in your life experiences. Robert Wilde from Bedford, United Kingdom said, "I have always seen life as a very complicated series of interacting threads, and this obviously parallels the interlocking answers in a crossword, which you can often solve by singling out and solving one problem after another, looking at related answers for assistance, until everything is done. Sounds like a good plan for life!"

Themes

The majority of American puzzles work with themes. In these crosswords, the longer entries are typically related to one another through a common thread—a thread that can also extend to other entries in the puzzle. If you know how to deconstruct the theme, you may gain some insight into the other entries in the puzzle (making it easier to solve them of course). Here are some basic types of themes that crossword constructors use in creating puzzles:

- All of the theme entries relate to a certain subject, such as a commemorative puzzle related to a celebrity.
- The theme entries contain a word or phrase that relates it to the other clues. Perhaps all of the solutions contain a type of wood or color.
- The themed solutions contain puns related to a specific topic, possibly swapping out words in a phrase to make them all relevant.
- Each theme entry contains words or sounds that are swapped with other letters to form new words and puns.

- A famous quote, or quote from the author of the puzzle, is broken down into the various entries.
- Entries follow a rebus theme containing symbols, numbers, or multiple letters.

The ability to figure out the theme entries and the corresponding topic is a great accomplishment for many crossword enthusiasts. Some solvers begin working on the longer grid entries right from the start, in the hopes that those solutions will hold the key to the remainder of the puzzle. This gives them an edge and jump-start on the other theme entries.

The theme metaphor spills over into all aspects of your life. When you are able to keenly grasp the underlying concept of a task, career path, or your personal goals in life, you're bound to be more content and willing to follow that current. You'll be able to focus on the activity at hand, reveling in the fact that you're working toward your own specified outcome. It's when you go against the grain, against the theme of who you are, that you will find yourself unhappy and full of dissatisfaction.

Be Present

Once you have the crossword knowledge and strategies in place, it's important to learn that the exterior conditions can greatly impact the outcome of the game. When you're working through a puzzle, it is necessary to ensure that you are present in the moment and grounded. If you're an advanced puzzle solver, you can most likely complete a crossword quickly without putting much thought into it. But what's the point? Where's the enjoyment and focus to the task? Why not perform another activity if you are not at least appreciating the clues, solutions, and completeness of the puzzle? Sure, you may get some satisfaction out of finishing the puzzle, perhaps in a specific amount of time, but that's a way to appease the ego. Instead, attempt to please your subconscious, which is more concerned with your mental health, your stability, and the beauty surrounding you.

I'm sure many of you go through life performing tasks without thinking much about them. You drive to and from work taking the same route, but you may find your mind wandering halfway through the commute. Many times I have done this, eventually becoming alert to the fact that I have no idea how I arrived at this point along the highway, or whether I had been checking my rear-view mirror throughout the trip. It's a good thing that I never missed an exit in my semitrances, or even worse ended up in a car accident. But, it easily could have occurred; thus my point behind being alert and centered in your present state and activity.

When it comes to crossword puzzles, you're not going to hurt anyone if you don't approach them mindfully. However, you might make mistakes that could have easily been avoided. You may solve a group of Across clues that then provide you with the answer to a perpendicular Down solution that you didn't know, but if you're not paying attention you won't learn anything from that entry. Every activity, every puzzle, every answer can be a learning experience.

Practice Makes Perfect

One sentiment carried through all of the interviews I conducted for this book: The most effective way to excel and improve your crossword-solving skills is to practice. You can study the dictionary and the thesaurus, you can practice writing quickly and use shorthand notation, and you can learn all of the tips of the trade, but if you don't practice, this information is moot. Only when you're doing the puzzles, entrenched in the activity and powering through the solutions, can you learn your own methodologies and processes for completing the crossword.

The same can be said for any activity. If you want to excel in knitting, you have to pick up the needles and yarn and practice. If you want to be good at playing the piano, you need to learn to read music and practice moving your fingers across the keys. When I performed in theater in high school, the entire extracurricular activity revolved around practice. The repetition assisted us in learning our lines and making our movements and interactions with the other actors fluid and refined. The practices started as informal reading sessions, getting us used to our responses and our dialect. We then moved on to stage placement and using props. The practices culminated with dress rehearsals in full costume, proper lighting, and complete set designs. And then we were ready for our two or three performances in front of our peers and parents. We endured months of rehearsal and preparation, practice, and repetition for only a few hours of blissful attention and adoration.

Regardless of what you are doing, and even how much you enjoy the task, practice is essential in performing it well and with integrity. Practice builds on itself; the training that you undergo allows you to achieve success where you may have never dreamed it possible. Practice is a cumulative effect and is often necessary to allow you to feel pleasantly about a pursuit. I read in multiple places that it takes about six months of performing a new activity before it becomes a habit. It takes another six months for that activity to become internalized and a natural response. For instance, if you meditate infrequently and during your attempts you find that your thoughts are scattered and distracting, you may choose to forego meditation and discontinue the activity. But if you choose to integrate meditation into your life on a daily basis, working to let go of any wayward thoughts and interruptions, you may find that it's an enormously beneficial tool.

Practice is important. If you're making a speech before your supervisor or peers, it makes sense to polish the presentation before stepping behind the podium. If you're going to give birth, it helps to attend birthing classes to prepare for the event. And on a much smaller scale, if you're going to continue solving crossword puzzles, the best way to move ahead is through practice.

Solve Without Ego

Have you ever let a crossword puzzle get the best of you? You can't solve those last few clues, so you throw it down and storm off—angry at the world for the rest of the day. It's a useful tool to solve your crossword puzzles without letting your ego get involved and learning to let the anger dissipate.

Buddha's route to happiness was simple—just let go. The more you are able to let go, the more happiness you will feel. It may seem counterintuitive, but think about it this way: If you hold on to someone too tightly and they leave, you are unhappy. If you hold on to this moment in time with a tight grasp, you will be unhappy as further events unfold. The subject and the object are connected, such that when one pursues, the other backs away. When you are able to release the attachments you harbor so dearly, you will find it easier to cope when they are no longer around. It is impossible to hold on to everyone and everything around you. All living beings need to retain their own integrity and freedom. If you crowd and attempt to possess something, you confine it. This can result only in dependency and an act of rejection from what you hold close.

The same can be said for desires and goals. When you link your emotions to something you want, you become discontent and depressed when you fail. Your ego becomes involved, and you find yourself linking your own sense of self to the act of winning or completing a task. Emotions have no place in crossword-puzzle solving. Don't take a crossword puzzle personally. It is an inanimate object and has no desire to get you. Always remember that the puzzle is a hobby, and, like Zen, simple is always better. Stop looking beyond the clues and words for a meaning to your life that isn't there. Rather enjoy the journey and the outcome that results.

The Zen term mushotoku means without desire for gain or profit, without any goal. Zen meditation is supposed to be practiced mushotoku. When solving crossword puzzles, it is fine to have the desire to enjoy the activity, but in the true sense of Zen, you should not have the goal of winning. You can play just for the sake of playing and to luxuriate in the present moment. It is your ego that searches for validation in completing the puzzle, and it is ego that Zen seeks to displace. In *Zen and the Art of Making a Living*, Laurence G. Boldt wrote that there are other possibilities besides striving to win the game. "Be awake to choice," he wrote. "Remember you are the chooser and play. *Playing doesn't mean indifference.* You can play with commitment and intensity. You can play heroically and passionately. You can play with determination and perseverance . . . It really is true that it's not about winning or losing, but how you play the game."

This is not to say that you should not be pleased when you complete a puzzle or look forward to filling in the grid correctly. Rather the goal should be mastering you, being present in the process, and not about the puzzle.

No Clues?

Zen Master Kyong Ho quotes an ancient master, "'Accept the anxieties and difficulties of this life. Don't expect your practice to be clear of obstacles. Without hindrances the mind that seeks enlightenment may be burnt out." What if you came across a crossword puzzle grid, but you didn't see the corresponding clues? Would you become angry, searching frantically through the newspaper to find the missing page? Would you throw your hands up, declaring the puzzle unsolvable, and walk away? Now what if you were solving a skeleton puzzle, a type of crossword that actually gives you the solutions as the clues, in a list format, as in the crossword puzzle given in Chapter One. The goal of these puzzles is to place the words such that they all fit in the grid, horizontally and vertically, to adhere to the given layout. They are great for beginning crossword solvers and people who aren't up on the latest current events, language skills, and puns that it takes to solve many crossword puzzles.

Sometimes the solution to a problem is right in front of your eyes, but you don't see it because you're too busy searching for the clues. You're looking for the path when the destination is right there in front of you. And when you do finally discover it, it may not be completely intelligible. You may need to put the pieces together into a workable answer, one that fits all the given variables and solves the problem correctly.

Although crossword puzzles will (almost) always come with the corresponding clues, not every problem in life is so easy. You need to analyze the situation and search out the causes using the tools available to you—whether it's determining if your child has an ear infection by researching symptoms and checking her ear, or fixing a network problem across thirty offices by analyzing the computers, routers, and software. And when the clues aren't available or accessible, work toward the destination with determination and dedication. It will all fall into place accordingly.

Everyday Zen

One evening I found myself in the midst of what I am choosing to call a Zen event. It was 8:15, and my youngest daughter was distraught and having a difficult time falling asleep. I tried placing her in her crib and walking out of the room, but she worked herself into a fit of hysterics and called out, "Mommy." After a few minutes of this, I walked in and picked her up to rock her. I was anxious to get down to the computer and put in some more writing time before my mind began shutting down for the evening, but I knew she needed some attention first.

As I sat in the hard-backed rocking chair in my daughter's darkened room, I discovered that I had two choices. I could spend the next ten minutes mentally walking through the list of items I wanted to write about in the current chapter, making use of the time when I couldn't physically type, or I could simply enjoy the time with my daughter.

I choose the latter. I realized that I needed to accept the moment for what it was and enjoy it to its fullest. I didn't fight the circumstances and wasn't angry that I couldn't be completing my work, even though I was on a tight deadline. Instead I reveled in the small details. I focused on the weight of my daughter's chest on mine, her breath slowing into slight shudders as her cries quieted. I tucked her sweaty head next to my cheek, feeling it curve down my jaw line to the side of my neck. I listened to her slight whimpers and ran my hand along the contours of her back as I continued to calm her down. I felt her soft pink blanket as it pooled across my shoulder and down my arm. And I rocked, slowly back and forth, digging first my heels and then the pads of my feet into the rough carpet.

My mind was completely alert and centered on this one moment in time. Each night during the previous weeks, I had carried my daughter into her room and lowered her gently into her crib. I'd give her a quick kiss, thinking to myself that I missed rocking her to sleep, and then I would scoot out of the room, allowing her to fall asleep on her own. My subconscious mind must have known that I needed this night of soothing and bonding, allowing me to settle myself further into motherhood and cherishing this time with my toddler. I could easily see how quickly time passes, and I was thankful that I had that evening with her.

Try This

Pick up a crossword puzzle and solve it without your ego getting in the way. Don't time yourself and don't look to complete the puzzle a specific way. Allow yourself to relax into the moment and really focus on the clues and the solutions. Try using the techniques listed in this chapter and learn from the methodology of the crossword constructor. Invest only enough time and effort as is necessary and walk away as soon as you feel any frustration or discomfort. Come back to the puzzle at another time if you are disrupted or need to complete another task. Don't rush through the crossword just for the goal of completing it.

Piecing It Together

1 Tides
5 Ump
8 Wizard of Oz man
11 Zen stories
13 Corn serving
14 Single
15 Boredom
16 In the now
18 Shows off
20 Endeavor
22 Russian ruler
26 Much ___ about nothing
27 Net fabric
30 Lyric poem
31 Pen name
32 Half of a hand toy
33 Not down
34 Tell a tall tale
35 Energy unit
36 Geological time unit
38 3D space
39 Association (abbr.)
41 Topics

44 Rabbinical school
47 Instill new ideas
50 Potato state
54 Obtained
55 Number of commandments
56 Continuation of coat collar
57 Object Linking and Embedding (abbr.)
58 Medicinal resort
59 Fix

1 Augment
2 ___ voyage
3 Blackball
4 Put out
5 Honor
6 Garner
7 Worry
8 Foot digit
9 Lodge
10 Mesh
12 Farm storage
17 Supersonic Transport (abbr.)

19 Defensive covering
20 Revises
21 Concentrate
23 Determine
24 Spanish farewell
25 Stagger
26 Group who sang "Fernando"
28 Rice roll
29 Horsepower (abbr.)
32 ___ Olde
37 Goddess of war
40 New York City (abbr.)
42 Wicked
43 Lady
45 Dines
46 Dad's new wife
47 Pride
48 Unit for pain
49 Southwestern tribe
51 Short-tailed primate
52 Adult bird
53 Not young

Chapter Three
Don't Despair

A wonderful Buddhist saying states, "The arrow that hits the bull's eye is the result of a hundred misses." You perfect your game through adversity and failure. Look at failure as a lesson from which you can learn. Seeing failure as an opportunity for improvement makes it more tolerable and will help you relax and figure out how to go beyond your present level of performance.

—C. A. Huang and J. Lynch

When you make a mistake while solving a crossword, do you get angry and fling your pen across the room, adding another mark to a growing inkblot on the wall? Or do you take your oversights in stride, striking evenly through the letters and educating yourself on the correct solution? The Zen path has much to say on the topic of blunders and the growth of an individual. Mistakes are essential when it comes to moving forward in life. Mistakes mean that you are doing something, working toward something. In this chapter, you'll learn the best way to manage your crossword errors and how to minimize them in future attempts.

So What?

I'm sure you've made a few mistakes in your life. Maybe you called a client by the wrong name, or perhaps you broke your mother's favorite vase. So what? I bet you weren't expecting that answer, but that is the basic Zen approach to mistakes. This is not to say that you ignore your mistake, or that you don't deal with the consequences of your actions. Rather you accept the mistake as an opportunity to learn, and then you move on. Take the information for what it's worth—whether it's not speaking until you've verified the information, or walking with care among your mother's antiques. Don't dwell on the mistake, don't berate yourself, and try your best never to repeat it.

Lack of Preparation

Growing up, especially in junior high and high school, I punished myself internally and felt guilty over every mistake I made. I'm not saying that years later I don't do this still, but I now try my hardest to let go of my remorse over any mistakes and move forward. Looking back at mistakes I've made in the past, I often see that they helped me in ways I never could have imagined at that time. I grew from the experiences, and the errors steered me in new directions. An instance of this that sticks out clearly in my mind is when I was preparing to graduate college and was evaluating my choices for the future. I was relatively young, only twenty years old and a senior obtaining a degree in aerospace engineering at the University of Arizona. I loved school, but I wasn't sure if I wanted to spend the necessary years to pursue an advanced degree. I was itching to get out into the workforce and prove myself to the world.

As I often do, I kept both paths open and decided to take the Graduate Record Examination (GRE) to see where I could attend graduate school. I knew that if I could score high enough on the exam, I'd have the opportunity to attend the University of Southern California. I was intrigued by their aerospace engineering college and contemplated an emphasis on the study of virtual reality. Unfortunately I failed to properly prepare for the exam. I bought a book, studied it here and there, but never made a concerted effort to strengthen my skills in vocabulary and relationship recognition. The big day arrived, and I headed to campus to take the test via the computer. I walked in the cramped room and sat down at one of the five computers. I breezed through the quantitative questions, finishing them well within the allotted time. I then began the verbal portion of the exam and found myself at a loss for answers. I couldn't even comprehend the interpretation of the words, much less how they were related. The room began to close in on me; the warm air turned dry and hot in my throat. At one point I began coughing, a dry hacking cough that took at least ten minutes to contain. I barely made it through that section of the test, and with very low marks at that. I tried to blame it on the coughing episode, but in all honesty I probably would not have done much better with six glasses of cool, fresh water next to me. I had failed myself, literally.

I had the option of taking the GRE again, but when I contemplated that choice, I found that I really had no urge to do so. I could have remained at the University of Arizona. My grades and my initial GRE score were plenty to get me in, and I was even offered a teaching assistant position from one of my professors. But I realized I needed a break and instead began actively pursuing other avenues for beginning my career. After multiple interviews and contemplation as to which path I wanted to follow, I finally settled on a position with Ernst and Young, LLP, in their management consultant division. Consulting on management projects for large corporations was about as different from small classrooms and lab work focused on virtual reality as it could be.

So was my lack of preparation for the GRE a mistake? Would I have been better off continuing in the field of aerospace engineering instead of leaving all of that education in the classroom? Perhaps. Maybe I'd be a well-known scientist, opening doors to new technologies. But I choose not to think of it that way. I don't dwell on what could have been. Instead, I look at the strange path my career has followed—from consultant to project management to upper management to freelance writer to author. My life has actually come full circle back to the days when I would sit on the playground in fourth grade and write stories and plays with my friends. My dream was always to be an author, and here I am today. Had I studied for the GRE, I might not have achieved that dream.

Not all of my mistakes turn out so tidy. In fact, I'd wager that most of them don't. But I was given some advice from a friend that I took to heart and now apply to the mistakes that I do make. She told me that I need to feel the emotions surrounding the mistake, especially if there is any guilt involved. I then need to acknowledge my mistake and determine what the mistake is teaching me. Finally, and most important, I have to release the guilt I have taken on. I need to take a deep breath and imagine my remorse drifting away on the air I exhale. Then I need to move forward, acknowledge that I have faults, but also revel in the fact that I can overcome them.

Ode to the Pencil

On a much smaller scale, I've been able to apply this knowledge to solving crossword puzzles. Because as you well know, you're going to make mistakes. Many times I've accepted that first solution that popped in my mind and just knew that it fit perfectly on my almost empty grid. Unfortunately as I continued to solve the surrounding clues, I realized that my initial answer was not correct. So what did I do?

The first step is obviously to correct the mistake. If I am using a pencil, it is easy to erase the mistaken solution and write in the correct one. If I am using a pen, assuming it is not an erasable one, I have no choice but to strike through the letters and jot down the appropriate letters elsewhere in the box. To people who hate to make mistakes, the strike through is a glaringly obvious, ugly mark on the grid. It is a constant reminder of a solution that wasn't properly analyzed. Because they can't hide the error, some puzzle solvers won't pen in a single answer until they've verified the letters with the surrounding clues.

Learn from Your Mistakes

Author Philip T. Sudo once said, "You must take care not to make mistakes. But when they happen, learn from them. Use your mistakes as a springboard into new areas of discovery; accidents can hold the key to innovation." When you make a mistake while solving your crossword puzzle, correct your answer, finish the puzzle, but then take a minute to go back over the blunder in your mind. Review what you could have done differently or better. You can learn from every crossword puzzle that you solve. Did you spend too long on one clue? Did you get distracted while in the middle of solving the puzzle? Did you second-guess yourself? Did you quickly jot down an answer without comparing the other clues that worked in the surrounding grid?

Once you come to the source of the mistake, file this gem away and resolve not to repeat it. View it as a mental sticky note containing a situation to avoid in solving future puzzles. Don't define yourself by your mistake or consider yourself unworthy of the puzzle. Instead learn from the lesson.

Mistakes are negative only when you ignore the information waiting beneath the surface. If you are able to analyze the mistake, get to the root of the problem, and learn from it, you can turn the event into a positive occasion. Although a mistake may feel like a failure, it doesn't have to be one. Just make a slight change in your mindset. If you are able to learn from the error, you are moving in the right direction. Each failure, if you learn the lesson that follows right behind it, moves you further away from another failure. Once a mistake is over, toss it away and instead retain the wisdom that you garnered.

C.G. Rishikesh educates us when he told me that, "Solving crosswords has taught me not to take anything at face value, not to be stubborn about anything but be ready to backtrack, think afresh, and see whether there is not something that you missed earlier to see ordinary things in extraordinary light and extraordinary things in ordinary light."

Don't Blame the Cruciverbalist

I know quite a few people who easily get angry with the crossword constructor when they make a mistake or can't finish a puzzle. They're quick to blame the name at the top of the puzzle for their own shortcomings, saying the crossword contained bizarre clues or an obscure theme. That's not to say that a crossword constructor or editor doesn't let a spelling mistake or incorrect clue slip through the cracks occasionally. But in cases where you find yourself looking to place the blame of your mistakes or inability to solve a puzzle elsewhere, you might want to look inward first.

There's a slogan in the Mahayana Buddhism teachings that says, "Drive all blames into oneself." This doesn't mean that you should go around blaming yourself for everything and beating yourself up over your errors. Rather it implies that if you place blame on others, you are more than likely doing it to protect yourself. Instead of dealing with the pain that results from the mistake or error that was made, you are transferring the source to someone else. In the case of crossword puzzles, this shift of accountability from you to the constructor helps to alleviate any feelings of shame or self-doubt that may have resulted from your mistakes.

The next time you look to blame someone else for a mistake, take a moment to think through the error. Was it in fact your fault? What lesson is available for you to learn? And, if it is indeed someone else's error, now is your chance to work with forgiveness and compassion, even when you may not want to. Steve Manion, a prolific crossword solver from Phoenix, AZ, said, "I never ever get mad at mistakes, although at one time I used to get mad at obscure crossings. I assumed that it is not possible for me to not know one word let alone *two* words, so if I don't know *two* words, they both must be obscure. I have since softened my tone, but there is still some chippiness in me in that regard."

Are You Mistaken?

In Zen, mistakes are a method within which you can evolve. It's a way for you to cultivate your wisdom and humility. With each mistake, you become more aware of yourself, your ideals, and your values. When you become angry with your spouse and raise your voice, he might become defensive and lash out. When you are late to a dinner party, you may cause anxiety in the host and cause the other guests to wait for the meal to begin. When you are in harmony with the people around you, you will be aware of your mistake and the anxiety you cause. You'll work to correct the mistake, put everyone at ease, and resolve not to repeat the blunder. On the opposite side of the spectrum, if you are self-involved and self-centered, you will see only the anxiety and defensiveness of others as a backlash against you. You will become more uncomfortable, and the situation will escalate out of control.

If you carry the desire to be at one with the world, you can easily recognize mistakes and compensate accordingly. When you are in the position to give, you are aware of the times you are not being generous. When you are in the position to teach, you are able to easily discover when you are not bringing out the talent in others.

When you have achieved a higher level of self-awareness, it becomes easier and easier to spot a mistake in the beginning stages, and thus stop it before it progresses. Of course this requires you to focus on your self-discipline and stay alert. You also have to recognize, and eventually accept, that mistakes are small steps along your path. If you strive for perfection and frown upon any mistakes, you'll find yourself moving in the wrong direction. Perfection is what the ego covets and is a very destructive goal.

In *If Life is a Game, These are the Rules*, Cherie Carter-Scott, Ph.D., wrote, "Rather than viewing your own mistakes as failures and others' mistakes as slights, you can view them as opportunities to learn . . . Every situation in which you do not live up to your own expectations is an opportunity to learn something important about your own thoughts and behaviors. Every situation in which you feel 'wronged' by another person is a chance to learn something about your reactions. Whether it is your own wrongdoing or someone else's, a mistake is simply an opportunity to evolve further along your spiritual path."

Multiplication Errors

Just a few weeks ago, I was sitting down to solve a crossword. I sat scanning through the clues until I happened on 10 Across "Tempt (6)." I immediately thought up a few possible choices to enter in the grid—SEDUCE, ENTRAP, ALLURE. I decided to double-check the perpendicular clues before entering a solution in the grid. I glanced at 11 Down and saw "Goal over the competition (4)." My first thought was LEAD—as in the goal to be in the lead in the proverbial race. Thinking back on my previous solutions for 10 Across, ALLURE fit perfectly as the letter "l" was the second letter in that word and also the first letter in 11 Down. I penned in those answers and happily continued to work on that quadrant of the puzzle. I spent a good amount of time trying to fit other answers in, but I wasn't able to get very far. I found myself stretching to think very far outside the box and wondered what my problem was.

Then it hit me. I must have made an error with the first two clues I entered in the grid. I went back to 11 Down and pondered the clue a bit further. After a minute I thought of the perfect answer, EDGE. The *e* worked well with SEDUCE as a solution for 10 Across. I crossed through the first set of letters, entered in the new ones, and the remaining parts of the puzzle fell quickly into place.

It is easy to see how errors can quickly multiply as you solve a puzzle, no matter how much foresight you attempt to garner from the other clues before entering your solutions into the grid. When you write down one incorrect solution, often you can quickly add another wrong one intersecting it, especially when the clues are vague or the solution involves a good amount of commonly used letters. And as you're moving along, you'll find that the more mistakes you make, the harder it is to go back and figure out where you went wrong and where you need to make amends. You may correct one mistake and attempt to move forward again, only to find out that there was another incorrect solution that you wrote in earlier in the game. This even happens to the best of them! Steve Manion posted on the *New York Times* "Crossword" forum one Friday about his mistake on the puzzle that day. "The bottom was interesting in that the SW was quite easy. That didn't stop me from getting the first one wrong, causing me to go on a major-league wild-goose chase until I finally appreciated my error. I want credit for creating my own Friday masterpiece."

Escalating mistakes often happen in other parts of my life as well, both unintentionally and intentionally. If I find myself running late for an appointment, I tend to get anxious and rush through my remaining tasks. More than once, I have found myself at a pediatrician's appointment without snacks or diapers for my daughter. One time I was in a rush to get everyone in the car and on the road. I gathered the diaper bag and hurried to the kitchen to fill two sippy cups with apple juice. I was jittery about being late, and I managed to spill juice all over the counters and the floor, forcing us to arrive even later to our mommy-and-me class. It almost never fails that the more I am running behind, the more things can, and will, go wrong. I'm not the type of person to leave spilled juice on the counter or a pile of crumbs all over the floor, so any small mishap takes time to remedy.

Then there are those instances in my life where I've purposely made superfluous errors, in the hopes of correcting the one that I had already made. Those little white lies to get me out of a situation—blaming my brother for eating the last cookie or the dog for tracking in mud from outside. I'd pile one misjudgment on top of another in the hopes of soothing over my mother's displeasure. Of course it never succeeded and often got me grounded. Just as when solving a crossword puzzle, the more errors you compound, the more trouble you're going to find yourself in.

Embrace the Outcome

To some, finishing a crossword puzzle is better than leaving it incomplete, even if it does have its share of marks and mistakes. The sense of accomplishment and the mental stimulation far outweighs a bit of extra black ink on the page. Cynthia Stapleton, a stay-at-home-mom from Conception South Bay, Newfoundland said, "I am very meticulous when it comes to my puzzles. By this I mean I try to be sure before I actually fill in the answer." She will often cross reference the up and down cross letters to make sure that they come together before she ever touches the page with ink. "It helps to have a good memory in the way of letter placement," she said, adding that she is still pretty good at this technique, even though these days her memory is slipping. "In the times I actually do make a mistake, I will just cross out the word and try again."

Cynthia went on to say that she tends to write the answers she is slightly unsure of in smaller letters, allowing her space to refill the squares if she needs to replace them. "I try to do larger puzzles with a pencil because there is much more room for error, but again if I do not have a pencil handy, I will duke it out with my trusty ballpoint," she said. "In the times I do use a pencil, I still find myself crossing out instead of erasing . . . a force of habit I suppose. Cross outs don't frustrate me at all. For every wrong answer, there is a right one, and a messy completed puzzle is better than a neatly penned unfinished one."

Creativity in Mistakes

Research suggests creative people tend to make more mistakes than their less-creative peers. This isn't to suggest that they are less proficient or intelligent, rather that they try more than others do. They work on more projects, come up with more ideas, and develop more concepts. Some fail and some succeed, so ultimately they make more mistakes than those who don't try much at all.

So if you're going to make mistakes, doesn't it make sense to try to resolve them creatively as well? When you recognize a mistake, it's important to determine if there are any further steps to be taken. Perhaps you'll need to rectify a situation or address some wrongdoings. If you find that you are forced to redo a task from scratch or soothe someone's fuming attitude, it is necessary in the growth experience for you to do so with honor and integrity—and perhaps a bit of creativity. The object here is to expedite the education you're receiving from this error, and the use of imagination will bring forth ideas from your subconscious.

Even in crossword mistakes, creativity can be employed. Aisling D'Art, an artist and published author from Houston, Texas, tries to always use a pencil. In fact she gathers a real pencil (not a mechanical one—she is quick to note), a kneaded rubber eraser, and a pencil sharpener before tackling a crossword puzzle. If Aisling makes a mistake, she erases it. But in those rare instances when she uses a pen and incorrectly solves a clue, she goes back to the clue, makes absolutely certain that she has the correct solution, and then reshapes the letters into new ones. She does not cross through the letters, instead using creativity to meld her error into a solution.

Avoiding Mistakes

Once you've made a mistake and gathered the teachings that it provided, it's easy to strive not to make that mistake in the future. But, as much as mistakes are learning tools and should be welcomed in your life experiences, there are many situations that allow you to attain the information beforehand, aiding you in avoiding making a mistake altogether. Think about the training that you get when you start a new job, the classes you take to learn a new hobby, and the tutorials you read when you purchase new equipment. They are all essential, as the last thing you want to do is alienate a client on the first day of your new job or break the digital camera you just took out of the box before taking any pictures. As author and psychologist David Fontana says, "The only guideline is that there are no prizes for traveling quickly. Time means little in work of this kind. Rush ahead too eagerly, and you will soon find the need to go back and retrace some of your early steps. Travel at the right speed, and each step will take you, surely and steadily, to the next one. You still may find the need to retrace your steps from time to time. We never, in a way, outgrow the earlier exercises as we pass on to the later ones."

In solving crossword puzzles, there are quite a few ways to avoid making mistakes:

- Settle down in a location where you can focus on the puzzle. Don't begin when your children are running around, pulling on your pant leg asking for some milk. The more distractions you have, the harder it is to think and allow your subconscious mind to come up with the correct answer.

- Give yourself enough time to complete the task. If you know that you need an hour, give yourself an hour. When you find yourself strapped for time and rush through the solutions, you're bound to make a mistake.

- Use the tools at your disposal, if you're so inclined. Some die-hard crossword solvers frown on using crossword dictionaries and online tools. But if you're just starting out or need a helping hand, why not use them and avoid making a mistake.

- Think through the solutions before you enter them in the grid. Double-check with the surrounding answers, both vertical and horizontal. Then you'll have a good positive vibe and can put pen to paper.

Try This

Since at some point or another you are bound to make a mistake, don't cross through the clues as you answer them. If you pen through a clue and then later discover that you answered it incorrectly, you might find it difficult to reread the clue through your inked line. And the next time you do make a mistake, consciously determine the reason behind it. Resolve to not make that same type of error again and keep a mental tally to see how well the process works.

Scratch That One

1 Computer memory
4 Obtained
7 A type of moment
10 Epoch
11 Foal's mother
12 State of agitation
13 Typo
15 Pick on
16 Pallid
17 Trick or ___
19 Sun god
20 Imply
23 Italian aloha
26 Term of endearment
27 One to stand on
28 Respond
31 Coloring
33 Cooking measurement (abbr.)
34 By way of
36 Denounces
37 Audio player
39 European country (abbr.)
40 ___ and raves
41 Very little
44 Army knife
46 Hug
49 In the company
50 School groups
51 Married woman
52 Whichever
53 Type of sign language
54 High-school club

1 "Losing My Religion" group
2 Opera solo
3 Collect
4 Furniture wood
5 Vile person
6 Northeast
7 Asia minor
8 Masculine pronoun
9 Dined
11 An extinct Mesoamerican civilization
12 A.E. van Voigt novel
14 Cast away
15 Movie ___ & Joon
18 Crucifix
21 Camp house
22 Essential omelet ingredients
23 Meow makers
24 Institution (abbr.)
25 Harshness
29 Smoothes out
30 Rampage
32 Flub
35 Valuable items
38 Reckless
39 Small lies
42 Pack lightly
43 Unit of land
44 Southwest Airlines
45 Not lose
47 Bad (prefix)
48 Sixth sense
50 Pittsburgh locale

Chapter Four
Dig Deep

The obstacle is the path.

—Zen proverb

Cryptic crosswords are a very different breed of crossword puzzle from the standard ones that American's find in their local newspapers and books. Cryptic crosswords employ a different style of grid, and a unique form of clues. These clues are written using strict guidelines and result in a puzzle that challenges the best of solvers. The clues are rarely direct, and they usually involve letter and word manipulation. Here I'll discuss the history and defining qualities of cryptic crosswords, along with the lessons they can teach you about your own cryptic and problem-solving skills.

Hide and Seek

As a child I loved playing games. I remember lazy summer afternoons, getting together with a bunch of my friends to play charades or Pictionary on the living-room floor. On days when everyone else was at camp or off at the swimming pool, my brother and I sat down to play a board game or constructed our own with brightly colored construction paper, markers, glue, and scissors.

One of my favorite games to play both outdoors and indoors was hide and seek. When I lived in Traverse City, Michigan, the city where I was born, one of my most prized hiding places was in the back of the closet beneath the staircase that led to our basement. When it was my turn to hide, I snuck down the stairs and slowly opened the closet door, hoping that my stealth would help me to avoid the telltale creaking sound of the hinges as the door swung open. I held my breath and struggled to listen to the current number count of the seeker upstairs. I then shut the door and began to feel my way through the darkness, a black much more intense and complete than when I closed my eyes at night. It was a musty, heavy gloom that I knew only in that closet.

After working my way to the back of the closet, tentatively touching boxes and pushing cobwebs as they brushed my face, I crouched down and waited. The seconds seemed like minutes, even hours at times. My breath would come faster, and warmer. Just when I was ready to burst out of the closet and into the realm of game over, cookies, and lemonade, someone would open the door and find me. I wasn't a good hider. I almost always hid in that same location.

I was a good seeker though. I always had a plan of action, working my way outward from my counting post. I'd look through every nook and cranny, keeping an eye on the safe locale of our base so that I could catch anyone brave enough to sneak past me. I rarely had to repeat a turn as a seeker, which was good because I rarely made it safely through a turn without being caught when I was a hider.

This method of seeking lends itself well to crossword puzzles, especially cryptic crosswords. For those of you who haven't solved a cryptic crossword, you're in for quite a surprise. The first time I tackled a cryptic crossword clue, I stared in disbelief. I knew the rules to solving the clue, but it still was tough to determine which type of cryptic clue it was and what I was being left to decipher. As I solved the puzzle, I found myself looking at the answer key time and time again to learn the solutions. I didn't even attempt to fill in the grid on my own.

But with all things, practice makes things easier. I won't say that I am more eager to solve a cryptic crossword, or that I'm any better at them, but the methodology behind creating and solving cryptic crosswords continues to fascinate me. Perhaps the engineer in me would rather construct these fun puzzles than struggle through finding the solutions.

So What Are You Looking For?

Cryptic crosswords originated in the British newspaper the *Times* in 1930. The daily puzzle was set by Adrian Bell, who was among the compilers who gave these crosswords their distinctive cryptic style. He worked to create clues to deliberately mislead solvers while at the same time providing a perfectly valid definition of the true answer. As the years passed, a series of conventions developed, allowing solvers to recognize the elements of the clue.

Cryptic crosswords clues contain two very distinct parts. One part provides you with the straight definition of the solution. The other part is a word play that provides a clue by giving the syllables, anagrams, or the words that make up the answer. The two parts can come in either order within the clue, but typically they are separate and distinct with no intermingling. There is often an indicator word within one of the parts that gives the solver some clue as to what the word play is using. An example is "Defective in youth, kid around (8)." Give it a try; the answer is on page 64.

So what are you seeking in these puzzles? Well, obviously the solution, but the only way you'll do that is via the word play. The word play portion of the clue can be made up of one (or more) of the following:

- **Anagrams:** The most common type of cryptic crossword clue, the word play contains a word or series of words that can be anagrammed into the solution or a synonym for the solution. An indicator within the clue that mimics rearranging, mixing up, changing, or confusion usually signals this type of play. For example, the clue "Scrambled letters, a rag man" would indicate an anagram. When you rearrange the letters in "a rag man" you come up with the solution ANAGRAM.

- **Reversals:** This type of clue is a variation on the anagram where the word is written in reverse. The word may be the actual solution or a synonym in reverse, or it may be a smaller part of a charade or other word plays. For example, the clue "Slowing down, turned around gal" would indicate a reversal (from the words "turned around". When you reverse the word "gal" you arrive at the solution LAG.

- **Charades:** Just like the game of charades where a player breaks up a word into smaller chunks to describe each syllable, a charade word play breaks up the solution into multiple clues that describe the letters, syllables, and/or words within the answer, typically in the same order. As an example, the clue "Weep in front of the shattered picture, concealed" gives you CRY for "weep" and PTIC for shattered picture, resulting in the answer CRYPTIC.

- **Containers:** This word play consists of clues for two words that create the solution (one word within the other). For example, the clue "Doctor embraces isle, in the wrong direction" tells you to place the letters MD (for doctor) around the world "isle" to arrive at the answer MISLED.

- **Hidden words:** Here you'll find the solution hidden in the words of the clue. Indicator words for this include concealed and contained. As an example, "leaST OR Most" hides the word STORM.

- **Letter order:** In these clues, you obtain the solution or letters in the solution by pulling the first, middle, or last letter from a word in the clue. As an example, in the word play clue "last month", the letter we are looking for would be the last letter in the word month, or H.

- **&Lit:** This word play means "and take it literally." In these clues, the word play and literal definition are one and the same. &Lit clues are marked with an exclamation point at the end.

Other word plays involve deleting a letter from the clue, homophones, Roman numerals, palindromes, double definitions, and much more. It seems overwhelming in the beginning, but the best way to solve these puzzles is to practice. Seluna Bop from London, England, solves crossword puzzles six days a week and enjoys a good cryptic from the *Guardian*. She likes puzzles that rely more on word play and less on obscure vocabulary, one that is fair and makes her laugh. Seluna said, "When I started trying to fathom the cryptic, I was aware that I wasn't using my brain at all, and that I would inevitably be senile before the age of forty. I think using your brain can only be helpful in keeping it ticking over nicely."

Personally, I solve these cryptic clues methodically, just like when I used to play hide and seek. I start off by looking for the indicator word, as that helps narrow down the type of word play I'm dealing with. I then work slowly from the beginning of the clue. If it's an easy clue, the words within the clue are the ones being manipulated through an anagram, charade, or other device. I can usually pick out what words to play around with by first determining the number of letters in the solution. I then try to find one or more words within the clue with a letter total that equals that same amount. It's a great starting point when it comes time to jumbling up the words. Of course, if it's a more difficult clue, I first need to come up with the synonym or inferred word, and then begin to mold them into a solution.

And as always, I keep my eye always straying back to the base. I never waver from the grid and any other clues that can be garnered from previously filled in words.

Answer: BADINAGE—bad (defective) in age (youth) and it means to tease, or kid around.

Getting Beneath the Surface

When reading cryptic clues, the brief statement or sentence given may actually be cohesive and have a comprehensible meaning. Good cryptic crossword writers intentionally create interesting clues to throw you off track. Although a clue may look like it has a solution on the surface, it typically is unrelated to the cryptic solution that you'll come up with. You have to learn to ignore the first initial surface reading and instead search for clues. For instance

"Bad luck rag disrupts scoundrel (10)," could give you an image of a villain who is stopped by a blanket being thrown on him. But that is far from the truth. The word "disrupts" in the clue signified an anagram, and you can scramble the words "bad luck rag" to spell a word with the definition "scoundrel"—BLACKGUARD.

This knack for getting to the solution beneath the surface follows directly along with the Zen teachings. Most of us spend our lives in a constant state of chaos and scrambling—with a list of a hundred items that need to get done. The family is sitting at the dinner table waiting to be fed, the bills need to be paid, and there are expectations from everyone around us. If you are anything like me, when you do find a moment to sit down and relax, your brain runs a mile a minute, ticking through the list of demands and tasks that still wait unattended. It takes me a long time to fall asleep at night because my mind is constantly going, chewing on some thought or beating myself up over something stupid I did that day.

Unfortunately these ups and downs, these time constraints and deadlines, all keep us from delving beneath our surface layers to find out who we really are and what our purpose in this lifetime is. When was the last time you really asked yourself what you wanted from life, or if you were truly happy? Perhaps you're afraid of the answer, afraid of making changes, or you just don't have the time to dream of some parallel life. But ultimately that's what you need to do in order to understand yourself and be content.

Part of the purpose of the Zazen meditation discussed in the next chapter is to rid yourself of surface thoughts, allowing your subconscious mind to arise, observe, and understand itself. The goal of Zen is satori, which roughly translates into individual enlightenment through a flash of awareness. Satori is a moment of clarity wherein one awakens to the nature of one's own mind and the nature of reality. It is experienced as a spiritual rebirth and allows the person to acquire a completely new outlook on the world. In order to reach satori, one must understand oneself.

Grid Differences

Cryptic crosswords are different from American crosswords in more than just their clues. If you're used to solving American crosswords, the grid in a cryptic puzzle may confuse you. The first type of grid you might see is one with a lot of black squares. This may at first seem easy, considering there are fewer solutions for you to determine, but it could actually prove to be a hindrance because it doesn't give you many crossing points to double-check your answers. The same holds true for the second type of grid, which is one with no black squares. These grids define the solution entries using bars. The bars appear to look like a bolded line (or a squished block) between two letters in the normal lines of the grid. Sometimes only one edge of a square will have a bar, while other squares may have three edges blocked off.

The bars and multitude of black squares are common in British puzzles because they allow unchecked letters (called unches)—or letters that don't need to cross with another answer.

According to Richard Morse, an occasional contributor to *The Listener* crossword puzzle, "The unches obviously make composition much easier in England, but this is balanced by a more restricted vocabulary, which frowns on excessive use of proper nouns, abbreviations, acronyms, and even plurals." There are rules regarding the unches, and traditionally every other letter in a solution should be checked with another letter.

Cryptic Messages

In general, daily newspaper cryptic crosswords do not contain thematic material, even in the jumbo puzzles. Many weekly puzzles, however are specialist puzzles with themes. The theme is usually alluded to in the title, and the entries may be abstract or wholly related to one another. Richard said he once set a puzzle where solvers had to identify fourteen words that contained different anagrams of ENIGMA within them and replace those anagrams with the titles of Elgar's 14 "Enigma Variations." Yikes! Sometimes the diagram, once solved, contains a message that needs to be resolved or altered in some way.

Many papers in the United Kingdom print two sets of clues—cryptic and definitional. This allows the solver to choose the degree of difficulty they wish to pursue in solving the puzzle.

Lateral Thinking

I recently wrote a book called *The Everything Lateral Thinking Puzzles Book*, containing 720 original puzzles. As I began researching and writing about crossword puzzles, I discovered an interesting similarity between the two types of activities. Crossword puzzles in general, and cryptic crosswords in particular, can teach you a good deal about lateral thinking. Lateral thinking involves pushing your brain to think outside of the normal scope of workable solutions. It requires you to discard the obvious answers and instead come up with obscure possibilities. The term lateral thinking was created by Dr. Edward de Bono, a prize-winning author and public speaker, and it represents a process and willingness to look at things in different ways. He suggests disrupting your sequence of thinking to arrive at the solution from a different angle. Lateral thinking is the opposite of vertical thinking, or the process of thinking sequentially along the most-likely path.

In lateral thinking, you are required to check your assumptions and ensure that they are indeed correct, something you need to be conscious of when solving cryptic crosswords as well. Rosie Paquette said, "Cryptic clues teach us that things are not always what they seem on the surface." She went on to say that one word can have a myriad of meanings and that we need to keep that in mind at all times. "Context and clever wording can lead us down a garden path and trick us. The best clues achieve that beautifully. I suppose you could say cryptics teach you to have an open mind and think in unconventional ways."

Lateral thinking can also come into play when you're determining whether or not the solution to a crossword clue uses a single world or multiple words. Many crossword puzzles will signal a solution with multiple words in the clue by indicating the number of words or the number of letters at the end of the clue, such as "Leprechaun's morning drink (2 wds)" or (5,3) for an answer of GREEN TEA. But many crossword puzzles do not include this notation, giving you only the eight squares in the puzzle grid itself. This leaves you to determine for yourself whether the solution is one longer word or two shorter words, and this requires a good deal of lateral thinking. Instead of running through the dictionary of words contained in your head, you're now forced to remember witty phrases and multiple word titles. Instead of dealing with the known length of your solution entry, you are now thrust into the unknown world of multiple words of varying lengths with only the sum as a clue. Lateral thinking indeed!

Problem-Solving Skills

Along with lateral-thinking skills, cryptic puzzles can teach you a lot about general problem-solving skills. In fact, the act of solving standard (American) crossword puzzles can teach you the skills as well. When solving a generic problem, you will find that there exists a series of steps to guide you toward a solution.

The first step is defining the problem. In the case of crossword puzzles, the problem is relatively easy: You need to solve the clues in such a fashion that the answers adhere to the grid and the surrounding entries. But in other situations, the definition stage may take longer to work through as you examine the who, what, where, how, and why of the problem. This stage is the most important as it allows you to delve deep into the heart of the issue and search for the root source of the trouble.

The next step is setting your priorities. What needs to be done first and what can be done at a later time? In crosswords, you can prioritize based on the clues that you can answer easily. You may choose to focus on the longer entries or a specific quadrant, leaving the other clues until later. In other issues, you may have to do an intermediary fix so that the business can continue to run, or so that you can move on and concentrate on the other tasks at hand.

After you have addressed any immediate issues, you can develop a strategy for solving your problem. You may want to identify alternative strategies before deciding on the most effective considering your restraints. In solving a crossword puzzle, you can create your own strategies for solving—using the clues and grid to best suit your style. In other problems, you may wish to research various options, speaking to others who have been in the same situation.

Now it's time to get started. Move forward, monitoring your actions against your plan and keep track of any success indicators. It's helpful to stay where the energy is, so once you get going, stick with the momentum. You may need to stop and revise your plan if you find that the problem is not being addressed or other issues are occurring as a result.

Lastly you want to verify that the problem has been resolved. In solving a crossword, you can easily crosscheck your answers with the solution or by ensuring that the perpendicular clues fit accordingly. Make sure to evaluate your performance and learn from the experience. If you learned a new definition or clue, file it away for future use.

You can use this method to walk through a variety of problems—crossword puzzles, family conflicts, work mishaps, corporate consulting, and much more. The more frequently you follow the problem-solving process, the easier it will become. It will be second nature for you to think through your strategies before jumping into a solution head on. The skill set necessary to have patience and foresight are imperative to leading a fulfilling life full of awareness.

Try This

If you haven't tried a cryptic crossword, pick one up. They can be found in *GAMES* magazine, the *Guardian*, and many other places. Don't expect to complete it on the first try, rather take your time and check the solutions when you get stuck. You'll really have to practice these in order to discover the methodologies and nuances of the trade. Many people start by first determining if any of the words or phrases can be anagrammed, often writing the letters in different orders on a scratch piece of paper to find possible solutions. From there they can find the definition and hopefully the answer.

Twister

7 Doctor embraces
isle, in the
wrong direction

8 Show her heart-
less, baby party

9 Home diamond
conceals, public
information

10 Weep in front
of the shattered
picture, con-
cealed

12 Scrambled let-
ters, a rag man

14 Wedding neces-
sity, blending the
middle engine
tying a boat up
backward

16 Advantage,
looking within
instead

18 Spies do turn on
you, get rid of
evidence

21 Hold, a quarter
perhaps sur-
rounding a dis-
orderly tan

22 Remove the top
of the head

25 Untamed Prime
Minister

26 Angered saltan,
obliquely

1 Even hair dyer,
doesn't want to
be found

2 Crazy gin lug,
sticking together

3 Lyrical poem,
missing mode

4 Silly stars, beam-
ing emperors

5 Jumping bean
frog

6 Half mortal off-
spring, Heracles
and Thiseas

11 Slowing down,
turned around
gal,

13 Conceptual, scat-
tered inn loot

15 Fruit annoyance,
revoked tip

17 Stolen ashtray,
wrong way

19 Plucked duck
within a pile,
salty carnival
treat

20 Pressed juice,
firstborn cat on a
windy ride

23 Hidden Zulu
name, moon
Goddess

24 Nocturnal mam-
mal, odd beast.

Chapter Five

Relax and Take a Deep Breath

When you think of it, anything done mindfully and with a certain attitude can be a spiritual practice. One of the key indicators of a rich spiritual life is this quality of mindfulness in all activities—playing close attention to what you are doing, and in the act of immersing yourself in the mindfulness, turning off the nonstop chattering in your head.
—Bernadette Murphy, *Zen and the Art of Knitting*

Meditation is essential to the Zen philosophy and can, and should, be easily integrated into your crossword-solving routine. Meditation is a proven way to bring about mental calmness and relaxation by suspending the river of thoughts that typically cascade through your mind. Meditation is a useful tool to center your awareness on the present and awaken your subconscious, a fabulous mechanism for finding crossword solutions. Meditation is also a method to reduce stress and elevate your mood.

What Is Meditation?

According to Joan Borysenko, Ph.D., author of *Minding the Body, Mending the Mind*, meditation can be broadly defined as an activity that keeps the attention pleasantly anchored in the now.

When your mind is calm and focused in the present, it is not reacting to memories and events from the past or preoccupying itself with thoughts and plans for the future. "Meditation," Dr. Borysenko said, "helps to keep us from identifying with the 'movies of the mind.'"

Zen meditation is a very specific practice that goes by the name Zazen—a term that combines the word za (to sit) with Zen (meditation). The term is deceptively simple. Zazen is a practice to settle your mind in its original state so that you can see the world with clarity and purity. It is the study of the self. It is the unlearning of everything you have learned up to this point. It is not the act of retreating into oneself—rather it is being still, open, and receptive. The great Master Dogen, a zen master and author from the 13th century, once said, "To study the Buddha way is to study the self, to study the self is to forget the self, and to forget the self is to be enlightened by the ten thousand things." In Zazen, the body, breath, and mind come together as one.

There are specific postures used when participating in a Zazen meditation. The traditional position is in lotus where you are seated on the floor with your legs crossed like a pretzel in front of you. This sitting posture allows the body to be in its natural state. The shoulders are relaxed, releasing any tension, and the weight is evenly balanced. Your center is rooted in the lower abdomen, and your weight is forward of the sit-bones (where your femur meets your pelvis). Your chin is tucked in to tip your spine forward, and you are focused on elongating your spine as if it were being stretched from both ends. The spinal cord is erect, but not stiff. Your vision focal point is on the ground about six feet in front of you.

Once in position, you shut your mouth lightly and breathe normally through your nose, counting your breaths in sets of fives (or tens). Each inhale and exhale together equals one count. When you reach the fifth breath, you count backward again to one. Try to draw your breath gently and deeply into the hara, the area of your body about two inches below the navel. The hara is very important in Zen. It is a source of energy and the center of your attentiveness. Subjectively speaking, the hara is where man and universe meet.

After you have settled into the correct posture and are focused on your breathing, random thoughts will most likely begin to fill your mind. Your goal is to let those thoughts pass by. As soon as one comes, let it go. Do not follow it. If thoughts about laundry, grocery shopping, work, or your children arise, let them dissipate. Do not have emotions or anger toward the ideas that float through your head—and don't try to focus on not thinking, as that is just another thought to clutter your mind. In Zazen, the central concentration is on your posture, breath, and attitude. Everything else should be allowed to dissipate, allowing the awareness in your subconscious to rise to the surface and finally be expressed. The ultimate goal (although I hesitate to use the word goal, as the Zen philosophy frowns on the use of goal setting) of Zazen is to control the ego and receive enlightenment. This is not necessarily an easy task, but it's the fundamental desired outcome nonetheless.

The more you practice Zazen, the more you will find that the time stretches endlessly. Twenty minutes may feel like hours. Beware of meditation time that seems to fly by. The goal is not to waste the minutes, rather to learn from them.

Parmesan Cheese and Toilet Paper

The same process of allowing your subconscious to emerge and provide insight and clarity can often be seen when you're solving crossword puzzles. I can't even begin to count the number of times that I've sat down to solve a crossword only to find that my mind was elsewhere. I'd think about adding Parmesan cheese and toilet paper to my grocery list or worry about a writing deadline that was fast approaching the following week. I would begin skimming the clues, only to discover halfway through the list that I hadn't actually processed any of them. I'd then backtrack to the beginning and start over. The second time around, once I became immersed in the puzzle, the answers came to me quickly and easily. Like Zazen, when I cleared the surface thoughts and distractions, my subconscious easily processed the puzzle, letting thoughts and answers caught deep in the recesses of my mind come forth.

Your subconscious mind often holds the answers to the clues you just can't seem to solve. If you, in the words of the philosopher Chang-tzu, "Let your mind wander in simplicity, blend your spirit with the vastness, follow along with things the way they are, and make no room for personal views," you may find that by pushing away the peripheral thoughts, you have easier access to a wealth of information. You can visualize the clue and then ask your subconscious to bring forward the solution. You may not receive the information at that moment in time, but you will set your inner mind to work and hopefully arrive at the solution shortly.

Accessing the Subconscious

Although the subconscious holds a wealth of information, it is often difficult to find a way to access it. When mastering the form of Rinzai Zen, one of the two major Japanese Zen sects, monks are given koans to contemplate while they are meditating. A koan is a story, question, statement, or dialog related to the history of Zen. They are sometimes viewed as impossible problems without solutions. They appear to be paradoxical, but this is said to be untrue. Paradoxes occur only in the language, in the words that make up the koan. The koans go beyond the words and ideas and lead to an experience of enlightenment.

Koans are meant to reflect the state of an enlightened sage and historical figure, usually quoting his exact words or a dialogue with that person. The teacher-student relationship is extremely important in the study of koans. The teacher provides guidance and also checks for the student's understanding of the lesson. The koan is used to accelerate the path to enlightenment by shocking the mind into awareness or shifting the viewpoint of the trainee. The teacher pushes the student to use lateral thinking, looking beyond the obvious definitions and associations included within the words of the koan. The Zen master knows that in order to find the answer, he needs to still his mind and allow his subconscious self to respond.

This unconscious self is available to all of us; we just need to learn how to use it. Experts say that in order to access the subconscious mind, you need to use repetition. The Web site *www.enchangedminds.com*, proposes using puzzles to access the deeper mind, presenting it with puzzling situations that can't be reasoned out by linear thinking. The more you use this "muscle," the easier and more useful it becomes. Who wouldn't want their subconscious mind spewing out answers to a crossword puzzle at an accurate, and rapid, pace? Just as crossword puzzle–solving skills take time to cultivate and require much practice, so do lateral-thinking skills. If you find yourself becoming increasingly frustrated that the answer is on the tip of your tongue, but you cannot seem to access it, it's time to brush up on harnessing your subconscious. Pick up a lateral-thinking puzzle book or visit *www.enchantedminds.com* for a daily puzzle.

Trying to Escape

I know many people who meditate as a way to release the stress and trials of their lives, their families, and their jobs. They are not attempting to escape from their current situation, rather escape to their authentic self and their higher reality. They take time out from their days, whether it is in the middle of their lunch hours or right before they go to bed, to unwind, gather their thoughts, and bring themselves back to the present. Meditation is a proven way to reduce stress, anxiety, and depression.

In a parallel methodology, C.G. Rishikesh uses crossword puzzles as his means to escape into his own reality. He told me that there are moments in his life when everyone seems to conspire against him, and even his loved ones are in a nasty mood. "In the face of such circumstances, what else can I do but pick up a crossword book and gently depart from the scene."

Away from everyone, he can spend some agreeable minutes with a cryptic puzzle. "It's a distant world altogether, and the battle is between me and the compiler," he said. "As the clues fall one by one and the pieces of the jigsaw fall together, a sense of triumph envelops me. It is not only that I have emerged a winner in this brief encounter with a constructor but also that I have conquered anger against any person who raised my hackles . . . and there is also a sense of pride: I have done something that the person who infuriated me can never do."

Just Sitting

In Soto Zen, the other major Japanese zen sect, the primary focus and practice during Zazen is shikantaza. Shikantaza is made up of the words shikan (meaning nothing but or just), ta (meaning to hit), and za (meaning to sit). With regard to Zazen, shikantaza is the meditative practice in which the mind is just sitting. It is often referred to as the method of no method because there are no clear instructions for the meditation. You are not to think about sitting, you are not to think about anything. You are literally just sitting. In shikantaza, when your mind is calm and the thoughts and distractions have ceased, you can see the world more directly.

You will hopefully find yourself satiated with an inner peace and a harmony with the people around you. You'll experience each experience as it is, detached, with no predetermined thoughts or expectations. You realize there your body or mind does not weigh you down, you are just sitting.

Shikantaza can apply to other activities that you partake in mindfully. When your mind is intensely focused on the moment, on the activity that you are performing, you are engaged in shikantaza. It doesn't matter the activity--walking, standing, working, or solving crossword puzzles—you don't think about anything else, you just do it.

Five Minutes a Day . . .

Whether you are in a formal Zazen meditative pose, participating in a yoga class, or going about your daily routine mindfully, you are meditating and focusing on quieting your busy mind. I have made it a practice to sit down every day before I begin writing, taking a minimum of five minutes to meditate. I sit cross-legged on the thick olive carpet in our family room, facing the window so that the sunlight is directly on my face and not casting shadows to distract me. I close my eyes and take a few deep breaths. I then silently review my goals for that writing session. I move on to reflecting on my intentions for my life and my relationships with my husband and my children. Lastly I take a moment to breathe into each of my chakras (the seven basic energy centers of the body) and allow any thoughts to surface from my subconscious or the divine world. Just taking a couple of minutes to center myself before settling down in my office and typing away on the computer helps me immensely. I find that the days I do not follow this practice, I am more scattered, and it is difficult to focus. I end up checking my e-mail, or I get the urge halfway through a sentence to stroll to the kitchen to grab a cookie.

I can easily see the benefits of taking a couple of deep breaths before beginning the process of solving a crossword puzzle. Intentionally clearing your mind of distractions before tackling that first clue is a very powerful tool.

... Keeps the Doctor Away

Research shows that meditation has a positive effect on your psychological and physiological well-being. In fact neuroscientists have found that people who meditate actually shift their brain activity from the stress-prone right frontal cortex to the calmer left frontal cortex. This assists in decreasing stress, anxiety, and depression. Other psychological benefits include increased harmony of brain waves, decreased moodiness, improved memory and learning, increased happiness and stability, increased ability to handle conflicts, and increased rejuvenation.

The physical benefits of meditation include a decreased metabolic rate, lowered heart rate, lowered levels of stress chemicals, a decrease in cholesterol levels, improved air flow to the lungs, and higher levels of Dehydroepiandrosterone Sulfates (DHEAS) in the elderly. Meditation can also help to reduce high blood pressure as shown in an April 2004 issue of the *American Journal of Hypertension*. In an article published in the journal, Dr. Vernon

A. Barnes, physiologist at the Medical College of Georgia's Georgia Prevention Institute, reported that 15 minutes of twice-daily transcendental meditation (a meditation technique that requires you to sit comfortably, and allow your mind to settle into restful alertness) steadily lowered the blood pressure of 156 black, inner-city teens, and their pressures tended to stay lower.

Meditation also helps with various illnesses and conditions by allowing for greater pain management and assisting in handling anxiety in the face of cancer, infertility, and asthma. It can even work to build the immune functioning in cancer, AIDS, and autoimmune patients. Many physicians are recommending meditation to their patients and are adding meditative techniques to their practices.

Dada Vedaprajinananda, author of the e-book *Yoga Weight Loss Secrets*, shows how meditation can even help those people looking to lose weight. "Meditation is an activity that changes you from the inside out," he wrote. "Instead of forcing yourself not to eat the doughnut in between meals, the very desire to eat it will vanish . . . If you get into the practice of meditation, no one will have to twist your arm to make you live a healthy lifestyle, it will become your natural choice."

Working Meditation

Most likely you will not be in a Zazen form of meditation when working through your crossword puzzles. But that doesn't mean that you can't solve them while practicing working meditation. This type of meditation is a mindful practice—where instead of working to empty your mind of all thought, you are using meditation that is directed at concentration and a specific task. That task can range from solving a puzzle to joining with others to focus positive energy on a cure for cancer. Many people believe that groups working together can pool their resources, resulting in a magnification of individual energy that can literally change the world.

One of the most common forms of working meditation, or meditation in motion, is walking meditation. During walking meditations, you meditate on the activity of walking itself. You begin by focusing on your body—the soles of your feet as they contact with the floor surface and lift up again, your ankles and legs as the impact runs through them, your hips and the rhythm that ensues, your belly, your neck, your jaw, and so on. You then can focus on your posture and your breath, making sure to relax all parts of your body and breath regularly. You can then work to focus on any of your five senses and being fully present in the moment. There are many variations to the walking meditation that people incorporate as they partake in this process. Some choose to chant a mantra as they walk, while others revel in the beauty around them. Regardless of your object of meditation, the point is to become absorbed in the task and not to judge the thoughts and perceptions peripheral to the meditation that attempt to sneak in and distract you.

The process of walking meditation can be applied to any activity, including crossword puzzles. You begin by focusing on your breathing and relaxing your body. You then move slowly to reading through the clues and writing down solutions, all the while remaining in the present and not judging any distractions or mistakes. In a working meditation, there is no rush to complete the task. It is an opportunity to take care of yourself while enjoying the practice of mindfulness. You can pause to calm and refresh yourself when you find that you are tensing up over a particularly difficult clue or an error you penned in.

Instinctively, you may already use crossword puzzles as a meditative practice—without the processes or the thinking. Many of the people I spoke with solved crossword puzzles as a way to relax at the end of the day, or to escape the thoughts that regularly interrupted their quiet moments. Margaret Wood, a teacher from Perth, Australia, solves crossword puzzles to relax and to work her brain. "This may sound like a contradiction," she said, "but working on crosswords helps me tune my brain away from thinking about work or other stressful issues." Asaf Rolef Ben-Shahar, a psychotherapist from London, agrees and said, "I think they have a strange quality of both working my brain and relaxing at the same time." He also believes that crossword puzzles increase his trust in his unconscious. "I return to them after not thinking about it and find more and more previously unsolved bits."

Brain States

Your brain operates in various wave frequencies, based on the level of activity that you are performing. These four frequencies are beta, alpha, theta, and delta states. The beta state is associated with alertness, concentration, and cognition. You spend most of your day in a beta state, with your mind focused and processing information. The more calming alpha state is associated with relaxation and visualization. In the alpha state, you feel more at peace and are aware of your surroundings as your brain shifts from the sequential left brain thinking into the free flowing and intuitive right brain. The alpha brainwaves are most conducive to lateral thinking, creativity, and accelerated learning. The traditional meditative brain waves operate in the theta state, along with activities centered on dreaming and creativity. People who experience spiritual connections do so while their brains are operating with theta waves. The delta state is associated with detached awareness, sleeping, and healing. Your body is in a state of hibernation. These waves are even visible when one is in a coma.

Although meditation typically occurs in a theta state, working meditation can occur in the higher frequency alpha and beta states. When I asked F. Sneep, a student of psychiatry from Almere, Netherlands, about his views on crossword puzzles and their relation to meditation, he said that if you view the puzzles in a wide perspective, they could be seen as a form of meditation and, in fact, everything that requires focus could be a variation of meditation. "I am pretty sure [crossword puzzles] would work as a meditation. But only as a small form," he said. "Real meditation is total silence of the mind. When I solve my crossword puzzles, I don't think my mind is that silent. I think I am in the beta state (Highly alert and focused; 14-30 wave cycles per second). And when in a meditation, people are somewhere close to theta (4-7 wave cycles per second) which is close to sleeping."

Everything Can Be Zazen

After practicing Zazen for a fair amount of time, it can begin to encompass all aspects of your life. In turn, everything can be Zazen. In his book *Zen Questions*, Robert Allen tells the story of a young American mother on a Zen e-mail list he subscribes to. She "expressed her frustration that, because of her parenting duties, she never had time to practice Zazen any more. Her teacher pointed out that looking after a baby was Zazen, and there would be plenty of time for sitting on a cushion with her legs crossed when the child was older." Robert wrote that Zazen is "all about being Here and Now and expressing your true Self in the simplest and most direct way possible. The reason it is so difficult is exactly because it is just so blindingly simple."

There are many ways to meditate, and there are multiple forms of meditative techniques. It is up to the individual to discover the best way to introduce and include it in his or her lifestyle. Perhaps that method involves solving crossword puzzles, using repetition and mindfulness to seek answers deep within the psyche. Richard Morse said that although he doesn't meditate, he thinks there is a zone one can get into when gripped by a particular crossword. He also found that on a large number of occasions, if he goes to sleep on a difficult clue, the solution just "pops out" later, suggesting that his subconscious has been working on it all along. If you lose yourself in a crossword puzzle and achieve a high level of concentration that could indeed be a state of meditation. Vicki Whelan, a psychotherapist from Manchester, England, felt that crosswords aren't a traditional form of meditation because the mind is working rather than still, but it could be a "dynamic meditation."

Of course there were those people who thought just the opposite. A few of the people I interviewed scorned the idea of crosswords being a meditative tool. They said that meditation is about relaxing the brain, whereas crossword solving stimulates it. They couldn't understand the relation between meditating and crossword puzzles, and one response to my question about using crosswords as a form of meditation was met by a firm "errr, no."

And then there was an e-mail that I received from Ian Williams, a consultant who resides in Canberra, Australia. He said, "I have been known to fall asleep (in a trance?) looking at a recalcitrant clue!"

Try This

The next time you sit down to solve a crossword puzzle, take a minute or two to settle your mind. Close your eyes and take a deep breath. Imagine that any peripheral thoughts are grains of sand, tumbling in the waves. Let them sink further and further, acknowledge each thought as it comes, and then watch it come to a final resting place at the bottom as the water settles and becomes calm. Take another deep breath and open your eyes. Begin solving the puzzle using your normal methodology, but be aware of any distractions or unwelcome thoughts that attempt to creep back in.

Stress-Free

1 Gardening tool
4 Baseball star ___ Ruth
8 Horse food
11 "I got it!" moment
12 Bridge wood
13 American Library Association
14 Perch
15 Zen meditation
16 Uncooked
17 Body poses
19 Above a viscount
20 Be
21 Candle dropping
23 Status
26 One who darts
29 Cmdr of police force
30 Jazz instrument
31 Flatten
33 Take a deep ___
35 Chews with teeth
36 Spanish river
37 Part of a circle
38 Severs

41 Muse
46 Environmental Protection Agency
47 Chef protection
48 Boston baseball team
49 "Neither a borrower ___ a lender be"
50 Strange
51 Roman three
52 Dynamite
53 Garden of paradise
54 Special keyboard key

1 Fastening device
2 Buckeye state
3 Dines
4 Blast
5 Stone tool
6 Honeycomb walls
7 Sea eagle
8 Center of gravity
9 Winged

10 Small sailing boat
12 Sapphire
18 Rags
19 Died out
22 Colorless noble gas
23 Charleston state
24 Check
25 Showery mo.
26 Dit's partner
27 Time period
28 Move a boat
30 Walked heavily
32 One billionth of a sec.
34 Three-toed sloth
35 Toil
37 Decorate
38 Penny
39 Once ___ a time
40 Tangy
42 One of the great lakes
43 Eastern continent
44 Drudge
45 Leave
47 Wonder

Chapter Six
What Now?

In Zen practice, we don't ignore confusion when it appears; we actually welcome it. When confusion arises in our practice, it means that we have discovered something new. The feeling of confusion is an indication that we are trying to understand something. So welcoming confusion is actually an expression of wisdom.

—Les Kaye

When you get stuck on a crossword puzzle, what do you do? Walk away for a while and hope the solution resolves itself? Or perhaps you look it up in a crossword dictionary or ask your neighbor in passing if she happens to know an eight-letter word for supernatural? Finding the proper crossword solution can be a bit troublesome, involving some knowledge, tools, luck, and hopefully some friends with different interests than you. It's always nice to turn around and ask a colleague who that kid was who starred in *Home Alone*, assuming that she is a Macaulay Culkin fan. Here you'll learn the best instruments for deriving your answers, along with what those methodologies can teach you. You'll also learn a few tips to introduce when you find yourself bored with the easier puzzles.

Asking for Help

When I was younger, in high school mostly, I was one of those few students who never turned their homework in late. In fact, I typically did my homework ahead of time. I had the same math teacher for three years, and at the beginning of each semester one of the first things he did was distribute the homework assignments for the upcoming months. I'd grab a sheet of paper from the stack that the student in front of me passed over his head. I then held the paper gently, but alarmingly, in front of me. I'd glance through the assignments, mentally summing up the number of problems for each chapter, and immediately feel a sense of dread. I'm the complete antithesis of a procrastinator and just knowing that these questions had to be solved left me feeling overwhelmed and anxious. Even though I logically knew that I had months to complete the homework, emotionally I was in turmoil with the weight of assignments settling staunchly around me. By my senior year, I was enrolled in advanced placement calculus, and I resolved to dissolve these feelings, not through patience and planning—but instead with sheer stubbornness. I powered through the lessons and made sure to stay ahead of the class by at least a week. Although it annoyed everyone around me, I felt more comfortable at this pace. I was also determined to work through the solutions on my own, without the help of our lectures and practice problems—mostly for the fact that a daily lecture was good only for an assignment I had already completed the week prior. I used only the textbook to guide me.

As the years progressed, I learned to let go of some of that anxiety, although I still don't procrastinate when it comes to deadlines. And I also very rarely ask for help (just ask anyone around me and they're bound to respond in the affirmative). I may perhaps hint at needing a helping hand here and there, but I pride myself on being able to find my way through, around, or over any situation. I hate to show any sign of weakness, especially in my professional life. If I am given a task that I don't fully understand, I am quick to research it and educate myself on the information available. That's not to say that I don't ask questions. In fact when I worked as a management consultant, I very often sought out the people within the company who were most knowledgeable in the subject we were analyzing. If I came in on the middle of a project, I would speak to those who had already been entrenched in the project. I'd gather their thoughts and suggestions and move forward with any information I was able to obtain on my own. I'd compile all of the sources and come up with the best possible solution. But I rarely asked for help completing the project, unless I had a team to work it through with me.

When it comes to research and finding solutions in my current career, I use multiple tools at my disposal. As a writer, one of my favorite ways to gather subject matter is to interview people, an activity that I thoroughly enjoy. I like to get them to think about the topic as I work to dig out any answers that are of interest to the theme or my readers. The automatic, surface-level answers are of little use to me, especially if the interviewee is well known and has already undergone multiple questionings. I want the juicy information—those roots lying just beneath the surface of the cover story.

Due to my appetite for knowledge and aptitude for research, I have no qualms whatsoever in reaching for a tool to help me solve a crossword puzzle. Heck, if the solution is available, that's the first place I will check if I'm stumped. I don't consider it cheating (although many people will beg to differ) because I am still learning. I don't just fill in the answer and move on to the next one. I take a minute to determine why that answer was correct and why I didn't recognize it before looking it up. Was it a pun? Was it a cryptic solution? Was it a definition I had not heard of before? The important task for me is to learn from the puzzle, to better my solving skills and internal dictionary—not to complete the puzzle without any help. Maybe somewhere along the line I will have that as a goal, but that time is not now.

Surrounded by Books

So when it comes to crossword help, what are your choices? Where can you go? When you're solving a puzzle and find yourself stuck on completing the solution to a clue, there are many books you can look to—the dictionary, a thesaurus, an encyclopedia, or even reference books specifically suited to crossword puzzles. These crossword dictionaries provide alphabetized lists of clues and their potential solutions. Many of them go even further and provide a letter count next to each answer to assist you in quickly finding the ones that suit your specific grid.

Dictionaries are probably the most popular tools because they are compact and list a variety of possible solutions for many words. In fact, when crossword puzzles were at their peak in the early 1900s, the New York City public library had to limit the use of dictionaries to five minutes per person. At about the same time, dictionaries were placed in train cars to provide assistance to those commuters needing crossword solutions as they traveled.

Thesauruses are fabulous guides as well, as the dictionary doesn't provide you with all of the possible synonyms, which often make up many of the crossword clues. A thesaurus will quickly give you possible solutions when you search out the clue and discover other identities.

Encyclopedias and almanacs are the best choices when it comes to people and places. The dictionary and thesaurus aren't going to tell you Abraham Lincoln's wife's name or who the pitcher for the New York Yankees is. Unfortunately, encyclopedias and almanacs can take up quite a bit of room in your home, so you may want to invest in the software versions to save you some space (and expedite your search time).

Internet Phenomena (6 Letters)

If you've tried the traditional resource options, or you don't have access to them, where else can you go? Google of course, or your search engine of choice. The Internet provides a wealth of knowledge, and those strange definitions you may be seeking out, in relation to the answer you're hoping to solve. Just be wary of online answers, as you may find yourself looking at untrue facts and figures. The Internet isn't watched over by any particular truth-insistent entity, so ultimately anyone can create a Web site on any topic and provide a completely fictional account of the facts. Hopefully you won't stumble on one of those Web sites, but it's always a possibility, so be wary of answers until you've double-checked the other clues. Of course, there's always the chance that the crossword constructor fell on the same Web site you did when she was writing out her clues, in which case you may have a solution others can't seem to figure out.

The Internet also provides you with online reference material as discussed in the section prior. You can quickly search for definitions and synonyms and look up encyclopedia entries through a variety of trusted resources. There are even reverse dictionaries available, allowing you to describe a concept or phrase that gets sorted through the software to return a related term.

If you're hesitant to spend hours clicking through Web sites in search of your answer, another option is to use crossword software to help expedite the process. Web sites like *www.oneacross .com* are available for free online, while other programs, like TEA Crossword Helper, can be downloaded to your desktop for you to use when you are not connected to the Internet. Both databases allow you to type in a clue and/or a pattern for the entry that you are looking to solve. You can fill in all of the known letters and place an indicator symbol (typically a dash or question mark) to let the program know the positions with which you need assistance. You can place unknowns in every letter location if you need help with the entire word. The software churns through its database and returns you word choices that fit your criteria. You may not always find what you're looking for, but it's great as a first, or last, resort.

And if you're not connected to the Internet or don't want to haul your laptop out in the middle of your commute, you can always invest in a pocket dictionary or crossword solver. These tools operate the same as the online and computer software, just as self-contained units.

Bouncing Ideas

If you are working through a crossword and find that you can't find a solution with these traditional tool choices, or perhaps you just need a conversation starter, you may want to try asking someone else if they know of possible answers. You can ask the person sitting next to you in the cafeteria or the one riding the stationary bike across from you at the gym. Or you can schedule time to solve a crossword with a friend or family member. Although working through puzzles is primarily a solitary activity, some solvers enjoy filling in the grids with someone at their side. They are able to spend time together, bouncing knowledge and ideas off one another, while solving the crossword at their leisure.

Barry Haldiman, a computer programmer and self-proclaimed crossword nut from Lenexa, Kansas, cosolves puzzles with his significant other, Beth. Together they solve the *New York Times* Saturday, CrosSynergy Sunday Challenger, Creators Saturday Stumpers; the *New York Sun* Friday Weekend Warrior and Thursday Themeless puzzles, and any other really difficult puzzles they can find. Usually the solving is done with the couple sitting side by side, often in a restaurant. This works out well since Barry is left-handed and Beth is right-handed, leading to tacit, though not strict, solving sides of the grid. "This is a bit unfair since it's easier for me solving from the left because I'll have more initial letters and her more ending letters of entries," Barry said. "But this disadvantage is less on the harder puzzles, and she doesn't complain."

Barry and Beth also solve crosswords together on the computer with one person doing the driving at the keyboard. Barry said that this is probably the least fun way for them to solve puzzles, so they usually rotate shifts. Every once in a while, they work through crosswords while driving, with the passenger reading the clues aloud. Barry said that often in the tough puzzles it's easier to be the driver and come up with the answer without seeing the grid, though he can't say why that is.

Another variation on their cosolving is when they sit across the table from one another in a restaurant. They use two puzzles, each solving a few answers (normally three) on their own, and then they switch grids. They continue swapping the two puzzles around until both of the grids are complete.

"What works so well about our cosolving is our differences," Barry said. "I have a bachelor's degree in electrical engineering while she has a bachelor's degree in music theory and a master's degree in photojournalism. This right-brain and left-brain help us get through some of the toughest parts of the tough puzzles. I'll get the sports clues while she knows the theater, etc."

Other crossword enthusiasts that I spoke to said they would rather spend time together with another person but solve their crossword puzzles individually. They enjoy the comraderie and welcome the ability to use the other person as a sounding board as necessary. Geoff Kirkwood, a mathematician from London, England, solves crosswords semi-independently with a friend in the pub after work on weekdays or during lunchtime on Saturdays for the weekend prize crosswords. "By 'semi-independently' I mean that we both attempt to fill in the same crossword but do not help each other unless we are totally stuck and even then the help is usually a slightly obscure hint," Geoff said. Mechanically, Geoff starts by attempting to solve the across clues in order, followed by the down clues, and then fills in the remainder looking first at clues and then checking with the letters. "It is uncanny the number of times that one of us solves a clue and announces that fact and then instantly the other solves it as well, even if we both had been staring at the same clue for quite some time."

Crosswordese

Another tool to help in your crossword journey is to know some of the crosswordese, or commonly used crossword words found in puzzle entries. These words are popular, not for their punny clues or fabulous definitions, but rather because they make good use of common letters and help a constructor to fill in the grid. Many crossword enthusiasts, constructors, and editors frown on these entries, but you're still bound to see them pop up where you least expect it. Some common four-letter words and their definitions are listed below.

- Abut—share a common boundary
- Amat—Amo, amas, ___ (to love in Latin)
- Anoa—a small buffalo
- Ansu—apricot
- Arte—French/German television arts network
- Baht—basic unit of currency in Thailand.
- Ense—an Anglo-Saxon slave
- Erne—a sea eagle
- Etui—a case for holding small articles or toiletries
- ITEA—International Technology Education Association
- Mene—ancient word written on a palace wall in Babylon, or the sculptor Pierre Jules
- Tern—another sea bird
- Unau—sloth

Although crosswordese typically refers to uncommon words, you'll also find that everyday terms creep up with strange and unique clues. I had the pleasure of speaking with Maura Jacobson on the phone one afternoon while my daughters were napping. Maura has created well over a thousand crossword puzzles for *New York* magazine, having constructed the puzzle for their weekly publication for more than twenty-five years. She has also contributed a puzzle to every American Crossword Puzzle

Tournament since it began in 1978. After discussing some of her crossword constructing habits, I asked Maura if she ever reuses the clues, considering all of the puzzles she has written. I was curious to know if she feels that it would be a negative to the fan base that she's accumulated, sort of giving them an edge. "Of course clues have to be repeated on words that reappear after twenty-five years at *New York* magazine," Maura said. "Many words reappear, especially three-letter words like ERR, ERA, and words beginning with A and ending in E. However, I do keep a list of the clues I've used for repeater words and have at least a dozen for each of the words above so that the closeness of repeats is usually many months apart, and hopefully they do not sound familiar to the solver."

Just Plain Stuck

What if you've exhausted all of your research options, or you don't have anything available to help you? What if the answer continues to elude you, although you know it's buried somewhere in your brain? What to do? Some psychologists believe that left-brain thinking, including trying to remember the meaning of a word or a synonym for a clue, might trigger a rightward lateral eye movement (LEM). Similarly, right-brain thinking often triggers a leftward LEM. LEM occurs when there is activity in one of the brain hemispheres that spreads into the eye field and controls eye movement. This often occurs when the brain is working hard to devise a solution, and the eye movement is actually a way to block out distractions. So how does this benefit you? Working in reverse, you can try looking to the right when you're attempting to search your memory for the proper answer. You may just find the solution staring right back at you.

And if you don't, you can always put the puzzle down, walk away for a while—maybe even a couple of days—and see if the answer comes to you. This may seem extreme, but some crossword enthusiasts refuse to pick up a book, or the solution to the crossword, until the puzzle is complete. If you find yourself in this situation, either by choice or because you have no tools available, think about the clue for a minute and then take a break. Let your subconscious chew on the puzzle while you engross yourself in another activity or a restful sleep. Pick up the crossword puzzle at a later time and see what your inner mind has figured out. Simon Chillingworth, a corporate planner and strategist from Wolverhampton, United Kingdom, believes that when you "switch to thinking about something else, you can often solve what was previously problematical." "Overnight, inspiration often strikes," Simon said.

Bored, Bored, Bored

Although the average solver of crossword puzzles rarely gets bored with a grid, there are some gurus who solve the *New York Times* Monday puzzle in less than three minutes and find that they are bored with these "easier puzzles." In response, Will Shortz, puzzles editor for the *New York Times*, offered up the following advice and ideas on the *New York Times* "Daily Crossword" forum for people who feel that a particular crossword is too easy to be fun. First he suggests covering up the Across clues and trying to complete the puzzle using just the Downs. "I solve others' puzzles this way, and the challenge is very satisfying," he said. Second he recommends timing yourself and then trying to increase your solving speed. "If you can beat three minutes on a Monday puzzle, go for 2:45. Keep shaving seconds off your personal best."

Will went on to say that there are other mental challenges you can play around with when solving the puzzles. "One expert I know fills in only the letters of every other column," he said. "The intervening letters must be kept in the head. Someone else I know does the whole puzzle mentally, without filling in any letters at all. A good way to build powers of concentration. And a good friend of mine never fills in any answer that doesn't cross another filled-in answer. Doing this isn't always as easy as it sounds. Using your ingenuity, any crossword can be made challenging!"

Spilling Over

The art of researching and finding solutions applies to many other areas of your life. When you are faced with an undertaking and can't find the answers within, it's essential that you know where, and to whom, you can turn. Even people who study the Zen methods and work to become enlightened have assistance with their Zen masters and through the koans that they decipher. Although you will not necessarily turn to a dictionary or almanac to find an answer when you are faced with a new job assignment, solving crossword puzzles can help you work through the methodologies of research and working to find a solution. These processes spill over into future situations, encouraging you to move forward with accuracy and confidence, using all of the available resources to meet your goal effectively.

Try This

The next time you find yourself muddled over a crossword clue, resort to a different resource than the one you typically flock to. If you're used to looking immediately at the solution, try to find the solution in a dictionary or thesaurus. If you normally grab one of the research books piled near your desk, try to Google the clue and see what results quickly appear on your screen. You may find a new technique to help you better your crossword-solving skills. Or you may find that you don't need any help at all!

S.O.S.

1 Phonetic S
4 Curdled soy milk
8 Star ___
12 Imitate
13 Desired cards
14 Assist
15 Google's services
17 Poison ivy result
18 French puff pastry
19 Dried-up
20 Web locale
21 Goddess of mischief
22 Male pals
24 Wail
25 Disks
28 Dictionary or thesaurus
32 Accelerated Free Fall
33 Internal Revenue Service
34 Simply
35 Total finance charge as a percentage
36 Geeky person
38 Baseball stats
40 Anyone
43 Passing trends
44 Public computer network
45 To sand down
46 Eroded
47 Large, flightless Australian bird
48 Region
49 Uncollected
50 Tai synonym

1 Soothe
2 A specification
3 Closes in
4 Implied
5 Orange-yellow color
6 Dues
7 United States Ship initials
8 ___ Stooges
9 Behind
10 Other
11 Kilometers per hour
16 Lift up
19 Eye infection
21 Curve
22 Victoria's Secret product
23 Game official
24 Nervous system
25 Overlooked
26 Department of Labor
27 View from Earth
29 Shreds
30 Goof
31 Destructive insect
35 In the water
36 ___ Dame
37 Correct text
38 Brunette or blond
39 Stationary
40 Frosty necessity
41 National Electrical Manufacturers' Association (abbr.)
42 French case
43 Future Farmers of America (abbr.)
44 ___ Jima

Chapter Seven

A Crossword Is Born

The most beautiful thing we can experience is the mysterious.
It is the source of all true art and science.

—Albert Einstein

L et's face it. As solvers, we're dependent on the constructors. Of course there are many cruciverbalists out there scrambling to be the next to see their name in lights, or more likely in the newspaper headline, but they each had to learn the ropes and start the process somewhere. At times I find it more interesting, and always more challenging, to compose a crossword rather than to solve one. I was lucky enough to have multiple constructors take time away from their puzzles to speak with me about their craft, a topic I hope you'll find as interesting as I do.

Zen and Creativity

When do you have your most creative and inspirational thoughts—when you're relaxed outdoors sipping a cold glass of lemonade or when you're running through the subway station frantically weaving your way through the crowd? My guess is that your answer is the same as mine, option A. I most often get creative urges when my body is relaxed and my mind is at ease.

These flashes of inspiration bubble up from my subconscious, but only at times when I am ready to receive them. Strangely enough, they rarely appear when I am searching for them. I can spend an hour staring at a blank computer screen, my shoulders hunched tightly up toward my ears, my forehead intent on creating new wrinkles, and come up with nothing. Zip, zero, nada. Later that evening as I sip a glass of wine and relax on a lounge chair outside, thoughts arrive, unbidden. Sometimes I get concrete ideas—ideas for a book or a new source for interview subjects. Other times I get wisps of an image—teasing tentacles that leave me yearning to follow the path and receive the full inspiration.

You have to be receptive when it comes to creativity. You can't be locked into your normal thought processes and methodologies. Creativity rarely follows a textbook. Creativity likes to tempt you, taunt you, and then seemingly arise out of nowhere.

When you judge your inner self, censor your ideas, and worry about what the outside world will think, you're blocking your creative self. The end result of this is an expression that is untrue—a work of noncreativity. You will find yourself unfulfilled and unsatisfied, perhaps yearning to give voice to the expression that is you.

In "The Art of Creativity," an article published in March 1992 for *Psychology Today* by Daniel Goleman and Paul Kaufman, the authors wrote, "The unconscious mind is far more suited to creative insight than the conscious mind. Ideas are free to recombine with other ideas in novel patterns and unpredictable associations. It is also the storehouse of everything you know, including things you can't readily call into awareness. Furthermore the unconscious speaks to us in ways that go beyond words, including the rich feelings and deep imagery of the sense."

When it comes to crosswords, construction is the creativity in the puzzles. The structure of the grid, the choice of theme, the layout of the solutions, and the word choice for the clues all contribute to the challenge that becomes the crossword. I hadn't created a crossword puzzle until I started writing this book. The task seemed extremely daunting to me until I found tools and templates for grid construction on the Internet. I downloaded some software and began my quest. The first few times, I played around and let the program fill in the grid for me. The results were okay for a standard puzzle, but I quickly determined that I wanted to place my own entries into the grid to theme them with the individual chapters. Maneuvering those entries around the grid became an interesting experiment in patience. It was often difficult to place the entries such that they intersected at one or more points, and I had to rearrange them often to get a coherent result. I also found that the entries very rarely fit into the template grids that came with the software, so I began creating the grid design as I went along, adding or removing black squares as needed to fit in all the entries and fill words I wished to use. When it came to the clues, I tried to keep it simple and not rely too heavily on pop culture and history. I figure such references are better left up to the experts.

These experts often develop crossword puzzles using themes. The themed entries are usually integrated symmetrically into the grid using the longest solutions (theme entries with less than eight letters are typically rejected by most publications). In a 15 × 15 puzzle, it is normal to have three or four themed solutions that account for 40 to 45 squares. The theme needs to be consistent across the solutions in order to give the solver an additional hint for solving the trickier clues.

Constructing Across the Decades

Len Elliott from Kent, Washington has constructed crosswords since the mid-1960s. His puzzles have been published in *Dell Champion Crosswords*, the *Los Angeles Times*, and the *New York Times*. Len was kind enough to speak with me about his experiences and techniques for creating a themed crossword puzzle. "I guess my first crosswords were constructed somewhere in the mid-60s," Len said. "I did three for my dad's birthday or Father's Day; I can't remember which. He said they were easy, probably pretty primitive, too. I can remember only one entry, OUTLANDER."

In the early 1980s, Len found himself unemployed, so he took time to see what he could do within the writing industry. Puzzles were a big part of his efforts, and he had several crosswords published. A couple of his contributions to Emily Cox and Henry Rathvon's *The Four-Star Puzzler* magazine now reside in the Anagram Hall of Fame—a collection of 1,000 famous and historic anagrams. Len's entries are "Reno's Damned Bait" for ONE-ARMED BANDITS and "Beatle Chaps LP Try—Super Song Blend" for SGT. PEPPER'S LONELY HEARTS CLUB BAND.

Len contributed four puzzles a month for three years to a Central Washington weekly in the early 1990s. Each month one of the crosswords had to do with a Washington or Central Washington theme.

After taking some time off from puzzles, Len got back into the constructing business in 2003. Since then he has had several crosswords published in *Dell Champion Crosswords* and one in the *New York Times* in July 2004. "The cry I let go when I got the e-mail from Will Shortz is still echoing in the house!" Len said. Later in 2004 and 2005, Len had puzzles published in the *Los Angeles Times.*

In addition to puzzles for pay, Len also constructs commemorative ones for friends and family. "In 2003, I made one for the conductor Stewart Kershaw," he said. "An Englishman, he had opted for U.S. citizenship in reaction to 9/11. The puzzle, as presented to him had the top five rows in red, the middle five in white, and the lower five in blue." In 2004, Len constructed a puzzle for a friend who turned seventy-five, and he also made one for Will Shortz, keying in on his passion for table tennis. "I did another in honor of my younger daughter and her male friend's thirtieth birthday, one for an office colleague who retired, one for my wife (plus a word search) upon her retirement from teaching, one for my 45th high school reunion . . . " and the list goes on and on.

I asked Len how he begins constructing a puzzle. "All my puzzles are themed, and all my puzzles thus far are 15 × 15," he replied. To him, this is the most fun about crosswords: developing a theme. "I have a thick file of ideas just waiting for me to refine them and turn them into crosswords. Sometimes I wake up in the middle of the night and start thinking of themes. If I don't get up and write them down, they're gone. Themes happen: a word, a thought, an ad. For example, the other day, I saw an ad for a fitness place. I've only got one idea for now, but it's WITNESS FITNESS." The clue would be something related to watching a workout show.

After starting with a theme, Len develops four or five entries that fit with that idea. These phrases will have somewhere between ten and fifteen letters—with pairings that will work in a diagonally symmetric diagram. Len loves puns and anagrams, so his themes tend to be designed with these concepts in mind. Ironically for him, the *New York Times* puzzle was pretty straightforward with theme entries of THE KINGSTON TRIO, THE RAJ QUARTET, THE TROUT QUINTET, and the entry DUET lurking around.

Len's next step is to look for a diagram that accommodates his theme entries. "Many of the top constructors apparently create their own diagrams," he said, adding that it does give them more flexibility in choosing theme entries. "I would rather spend the time filling the grid."

Len enters the theme entries in ink, and then works on the "fill"—or the words that fill in the remainder of the grid. The hard part for him is making the nontheme entries interesting and "noncrosswordese." Progress at this stage can be either swift or maddening for Len. It may depend upon the number of black squares, but sometimes he gets to a spot where nothing seems to work. "Then you have to quit, shift the theme entries around, change theme entries, or (and the top editors know when this happens) add black squares," he said.

Another refuge for Len is to throw in a Roman numeral. "I dislike it when I have to do addition, subtraction, multiplication, division or try to divine when an early Pope lived to figure out the outdated mathematical representation, so it's a desperate move when I use one. Another dodge is to use alphabetical sequences (ABC, XYZ) to solve a construction problem."

Len uses the software program Crossword Compiler to create the grids and assist with the presentation of clues for submission, but he doesn't use it to fill in the grid (which is one of the options available). He said it takes too long to eradicate the poor entries that the software includes, so he'd much rather do it from scratch. For reference materials, Len uses dictionaries, movie guides, almanacs, and the Internet.

A Quick Study

Ralph Waldo Emerson wrote, "Do not go where the path may lead, go instead where there is no path and leave a trail." If doing a crossword puzzle is following an exciting path—perhaps constructing one is going where there is no path and leaving a trail.

Deb Amlen seems to be running down her self-made path. I met her through a crossword constructing discussion online and asked if she'd be up for talking about her craft. Deb, a canine behaviorist and homemaker who lives in Springfield, New Jersey, chatted with me one evening in July on the telephone. Deb has only been constructing crosswords for about a year now, but she's already been published in the *New York Times,* the *Los Angeles Times,* and the *Washington Post,* and she has puzzles that will be released soon in the *Chronicle for Higher Education* and the *New York Sun.* Deb's debut puzzle, and only the second puzzle she had constructed, was an amazing Sunday puzzle in the *New York Times.* The first puzzle she created was later published in the *Los Angeles Times.*

Although Deb didn't begin solving crossword puzzles until she was an adult, she fondly remembers looking over her father's shoulder when he did the *New York Times* puzzle. "I remember watching him and being fascinated with the whole process," Deb said. "I didn't start solving myself until I was an adult out of college. I barely cracked them when I first started, but as time went on, the more I did, the better I got. It was a very satisfying moment."

After solving crosswords for years, Deb was very curious about how they were put together. She enjoyed word plays and puns, and her brain is always wrapped around these types of clues. "So I decided to try to make some money at it," Deb said. This was said in jest, as the crossword puzzle market is not a high-paying one. Current rates for the *New York Times* puzzles are $125 for a daily puzzle and $600 for a Sunday puzzle. Deb read an article about crossword puzzle construction. She looked further into the subject and found the Cruciverb-L list at *www.cruciverb.com*—a Web site devoted to puzzle constructors. She jotted down the address to one of the mentors on the board, Nancy Salomon. According to Deb, and other people from the list, Nancy had been mentoring members for quite a while and made it her business to turn out really good constructors. Deb contacted Nancy, who guided her through the process and worked with her on theme development, grid design, clue writing, and submission. Deb told Nancy about her theme for the Sunday puzzle, and then submitted it to Will Shortz. (For the Sunday puzzle the initial theme must be approved before the constructor submits with the puzzle.) Will wrote back saying that the theme was nice, but Deb should start off doing some 15 × 15 puzzles and when she had more of them under her belt, he'd take a look at a 21 × 21. Deb told Nancy about the rejection, and Nancy intervened on her behalf. Will agreed to publish the puzzle if the two worked on it together.

The rest, they say, is history! The puzzle debuted with the theme "Groomin' for Hollywood." Deb is a huge *Queer Eye for the Straight Guy* fan and folded puns on movie title names, based on grooming, into the puzzle. Some of the solutions include SHAVING PRIVATE RYAN, BATHMAN AND ROBIN, RAZORS OF THE LOST ARK, and PERMS OF ENDEARMENT.

Deb enjoys perfecting her themes. "Themes sometimes come to me when I am sleeping. Sometimes they can be sparked by something I read, or even a life event. Good ideas can come from anywhere if you're open to seeing them. I keep my ideas in notebooks. A phrase or word will get stuck in my head and get rattled around until I put it in a puzzle. Then it leaves me alone."

Deb's favorite entries are those using misdirection, or that can be clued using phrases that have a totally different meaning from the base phrase, like "Ticker tape, for short," for the entry ECG.

I asked Deb how many theme entries she likes to include in a puzzle. "On average, you don't want to overload the puzzle with too many theme entries, just as many as you can without sacrificing a really good fill," she said. "Most constructors try to generate as many theme entries as possible before deciding on which ones will actually go into the puzzle."

That decision is based on a few things: First, the theme entries need to be able to "pair off" in their letter count so that the puzzle will be diagonally symmetrical (if you flip the puzzle on its head, it will maintain the same grid layout). As an example, for a 15 × 15 grid, Deb might use three theme entries—a fifteen-letter word or phrase across the very middle, a twelve-letter word three rows from the top and flushed left, and a twelve-letter word three rows from the bottom and flushed right. If she added additional entries, they would need to have the same letter count and be able to fit in the grid accordingly.

Second, sometimes theme entries get sacrificed for a variety of reasons. "One could be an inability to find a quality theme entry that matches the first one in terms of letter count; another could be inconsistency with the other theme entries; still another could be that the editor just doesn't like it as much as I did. So it pays to come up with as many theme entries as possible to prepare for the possibility that some of them may bite the dust."

When I asked Deb whether she uses software to create her puzzles, she responded in the affirmative, although she constructed the first two puzzles on graph paper. Now she uses Crossword Compiler and feels that she's very lucky in the sense that she's working on a computer. She's able to do some research on the Internet, but due to its unreliability, she also uses dictionaries and other reference books.

Deb now takes about half a day to construct a crossword puzzle. It has become an art form for her now. "The most fun for me is the development of the theme," Deb said. "The puzzles that are 'meant to be' come fairly quickly. The first one took so long to construct, I almost didn't write another one. It was a big relief to find that my second puzzle didn't take as long. Working with Nancy really helps. There is a steep learning curve, but you come out of it with an amazing skill set."

Deb continues to solve crossword puzzles, although not as often as she'd like. I suspect that's probably due to the fact that she has two young children and a hectic schedule. She does solve the *New York Times* puzzles occasionally to keep her mind sharp. "It's also nice to know which themes have already been done before, and what's fresh and new," she said.

Cryptic Construction

Constructing a cryptic crossword involves a similar process to the standard American puzzles, with some subtle differences. Richard Morse, from Winchester, United Kingdom, walked me through some of the basic steps he follows in constructing cryptic clues, although he is clear to state that every setter follows a varied process. "Most setters keep a little black book (probably virtual these days) of words that might make good clue-fodder," he said. "For 'normal' daily puzzles, you then seed the diagram with a couple of these. They might include long or witty anagrams (e.g. MOTHER-IN-LAW is an anagram of WOMAN HITLER, so you might try to make a clue out of that!) or charades (for instance the two halves of DANCING-MASTER = BALL-BOY, which might be good for a clue in Wimbledon week) and so on."

Richard then fills in the remainder of the diagram, at the end finding that he is faced with a list of words that he wouldn't necessarily have chosen to clue. He works methodically through this list in order, but allows himself to bypass any particularly difficult words. He keeps a tally to the side of each type of clue, so as not to have too many word plays of the same type. He also tries to avoid having too many consecutive examples of the same clue type as the solver works through the puzzle.

Richard went on to say that it's difficult to speak about the remainder of the process, but he basically considers the following items for each clue:

- How can you define it? A humorous or misleading (but fair) definition is always a good start, e.g. "Number" for *anaesthetist*.

- What clue types are available—is there an anagram or an obvious charade, or could it be hidden?

- How can you join the first two in a way that is seamless and keeps the solver guessing? Richard said that "this is the real alchemy!" He said experience and "a deep knowledge of words and the (potential) meaning of words" is crucial here.

Richard walks me through an example, assuming that we're trying to clue the word READING.

- **Definition**—Reading has a variety of different meanings. It is a town in England with a university. It means studying, learning, or enjoying a book. It also means lesson, as in a Church reading.

- **Clue Types**—There are multiple ways that we can clue Reading:

   a. A double definition (because it has more than one distinct meaning)

   b. Anagram—"in grade" looks okay, although there are no one-word anagrams of the word

   c. Charade—not great, but maybe we can do something with E(nglish) + AD (notice) in RING or RE (about) + A + DING (=hit)

d. Hidden—possible but unlikely, such as "tREAD IN
Grapes"

e. Reversal—nothing obvious comes to mind

f. Other—Reading can be "treading minus its leader"
but this does not offer much scope

■ **Joining it together**—Richard feels that the best bet is
a double definition or an anagram. If he uses a double
definition, "University study" is a neat and obvious clue,
but a bit plain. For the anagram, "Studying danger, one
gets excited" where "one" corresponds to the letter I to
be anagrammed with "danger" and "gets excited" is the
anagram indicator.

Richard concluded that either of these clues would be fine,
and he would make a determination based on the remaining and
surrounding clues he is using in the puzzle.

The Maestro

After a finished puzzle has been created, most constructors send it
off to one of a variety of publications and bide their time waiting for
a response. If they are submitting a puzzle to the *New York Times*,
they are hoping to hear from Will Shortz, the current crossword
puzzle editor of the *New York Times* and often-touted King of Crosswords and Puzzle Master. I got the chance to speak to him without
the pressure of hoping for a positive reply on a crossword.

That day, Father's Day, dawned bright and sunny, lucky for
me as the past week had been dark and gray. Midway through

the morning I pushed my husband and daughters outside to play in the backyard and enjoy some sun. I grabbed my tape recorder and list of questions and walked down the hall to the guest bedroom where our speakerphone sits. I got settled next to the telephone and dialed Will Shortz's home phone number where he resides in what others have described as a Tudor-style home in Pleasantville, New York.

I had already read a good amount about Will, but I wanted to speak with him in person for this book. I recognized his voice when he picked up the phone, after only two rings, having heard him in his weekly stint as the puzzle master on NPR's Weekend Edition Sunday and also having recently seen a clip of him on *The Daily Show with Jon Stewart.*

Will listened as I provided a brief narrative of the book, and we dove right into the questions. I already knew that he's been the crossword puzzles editor for the *New York Times* since 1993 and is only the fourth in the history of the newspaper to hold that position. When he succeeded the late Eugene T. Maleska, Will made slight modifications to the crossword. He added bylines for the contributors and worked to broaden the cultural references, adding modern subjects including movies, television, and rock and roll. In his own words, he also added "more popular culture, deception, and trickery."

I asked Will what he specifically does as editor for the crossword. "The biggest part of the job is looking at the cross-word submissions that come to me," Will said. "I get about eight to ten puzzles for every one that I can publish. I get sixty to seventy-five puzzles submitted to me a week. The most important part of the job is looking at those, corresponding with the contributors about what I like and don't like. I do correspond with all of the contributors myself."

The contributors write the entire puzzle on their own, sending in a complete grid with clues and solutions. Will is a hands-on editor and ends up rewriting about half of the clues. "I will revise clues for lots of reasons, the most important of which is accuracy," he said. "I will check every word and fact in the puzzle that I have any doubt about. I also edit the puzzles for the proper level of difficulty."

I was curious to know what constitutes a harder puzzle—the clues, solutions, or a combination of the two. Will said that each puzzle has a natural difficulty level, and he can determine that from just looking at it. He said he can take a Monday puzzle with a simple theme and turn it into a Saturday puzzle, although it might feel forced. "It's nearly impossible to do the opposite because a Saturday puzzle has some difficult and possibly unfamiliar words, along with a tricky theme, and a wide-open diagram (more white squares)." He just can't make it easy, no matter how he clues it.

I wondered what tools Will uses to construct the clues. "I am surrounded by books," he said. "Dictionaries, specialist dictionaries of every subject you can imagine, and reference books on everything." He ticked off a list of topics including movies, opera, sports, cars, television, mythology, and food. "I have hundreds and hundreds and hundreds of reference books so I can look up virtually anything." He uses Google if necessary, but he prefers to use his books because he feels it is faster and more accurate. He also noted the abundance of misinformation on the Internet and said he's very careful when he does use it.

After he edits the puzzles, Will sends them to three testers. One tester rechecks every word after him. All three of them get back to him with what they do and do not like about the crossword. Will then polishes the puzzle and sends it to a fourth tester as a final recheck.

Will started working with crossword puzzles at a young age. He began constructing them when he was eight or nine on the Arabian horse farm in Indiana where he was born and raised. "My first crossword was made at the suggestion of my mother." She had a bridge club over for the afternoon and wanted to keep him quiet. She took a piece of paper, ruled it into squares, and showed him how to interlock the squares up and down. After the bridge club left, his mother showed him how to number the grid and write the clues. Will continued making crossword puzzles and sold his first one professionally to *Venture* magazine when he was fourteen. By the age of sixteen, he was a regular contributor to Dell puzzle publications.

Will attended college at Indiana University Bloomington and designed his own school curriculum revolving around puzzles. He obtained a degree in enigmatology (the art of making or solving enigmas and puzzles), the only person in the world thus far to do so. He went on to obtain a law degree from the University of Virginia, but he passed on taking the bar and began his career in puzzles. He worked at *GAMES* magazine for fifteen years and was the editor there from 1989 to 1993 when he moved to the *New York Times*. He has also been the puzzle master on NPR's Weekend Edition Sunday since its inception in 1987.

Later, I listened to the morning's show through the NPR Web site and followed along as Will challenged the week's winner to a Father's Day puzzle. He gave the contestant two words, the first could precede the answer to complete a compound word or two-word phrase, the second word could follow the answer to do the same. Oh, and each answer needed to start with the letters "pa"—thus giving it a Dad-like theme. I got stuck on a couple of the clues—"instrument" and "discussion" with the answer of *panel*—and flew through others—"foster" and "company" with the answer of *parent*. The contestant did better than I. Oh well, there's always next week.

Will founded the American Crossword Puzzle Tournament in 1978 and has stayed on as director for every event. He also founded the World Puzzle Championship in 1992 and remains captain of the U.S. team.

I asked Will if he still solves crossword puzzles. He was quick to say that he does enjoy solving crosswords in his leisure time. He doesn't particularly go for speed, but he does solve them quickly. "I'm obviously not trying to compete in a competition because I direct most of the competitions." He works one portion of the grid at a time, after finding a solution that he's sure of. He prefers a pen for a newspaper crossword and a pencil for a puzzle in a book.

I asked Will about mail from celebrities. I had previously read that he received a card for his fiftieth birthday from President Bill

Clinton, who is indeed a fan. Will chuckles, "I get it all the time. I get them for a few reasons." He laughs again when I ask him if anyone writes in angry about a puzzle. "That happens all the time," he said. He recounted a piece of mail he received from film critic Judith Christ when he began as editor for the *Times*. It was an "amusing note, not an angry note, saying that I was dragging her into the 1990s kicking and screaming." He then added that she eventually came around. Composer and lyricist Stephen Sondheim has written him multiple times, once when Will misquoted one of his song lyrics. Arte Johnson also sent him a note when Will used him for the clue "Jocular Johnson." The note contained only a one word question—"Jocular?" Will ultimately agrees with him that this was perhaps not the most appropriate clue choice.

One creative puzzle that I questioned Will about is the puzzle that was released on Election Day, 1996. The clue to the middle answer, across, was "Lead story in tomorrow's newspaper." Many people wondered how he could presume, and predict, that one or the other would win. What they didn't know was that the puzzle could be solved with either CLINTON ELECTED or BOB DOLE ELECTED. Either answer fit due to the ambiguity of the perpendicular clues. Shortz originally obtained the idea from the 1980 election when he was the editor at *Games* magazine. He received a submission from a contributor, Jerry Ferrell, who wanted to do 1 Across as either REAGAN or CARTER. Unfortunately the submission was too late to get in the bimonthly magazine. Will wrote Ferrell saying that it was a "fantastic idea," but he just couldn't do it. Sixteen years later Will was the editor for the *New York Times,* and Ferrell proposed to do it again. They collaborated on what Will now calls his "all-time favorite puzzle." His favorite clue is "It may turn into a different story" and the answer is SPIRAL STAIRCASE.

Try This

Create a crossword. Don't worry about the final outcome. Don't worry about the size of the grid and using themed entries. Just dive right in and get your creative juices flowing. If you want to do it the old-fashioned way, you can start with some graph paper and a pencil—or you can download crossword construction software onto your computer. You can design the grid beforehand, or see how it unfolds as you populate it. You'll definitely need some books handy, and you can use a variety of Web sites to choose words to fit your gaps. You can even purchase software that will populate a portion of the grid, or the entire grid, from its internal database. The only problem with the software is that it is limited to the word list that comes with the purchase, and any other word lists you choose to include, which could be a hindrance when it comes to filling the grid. Who knows, maybe you'll enhance your solving skills when you see the methodology behind constructing them.

A Blank Slate

1 Sheep sound
4 Pair
7 Knocks
11 Boxer Muhammad
12 Bequeath
14 Section
15 California (abbr.)
16 Pleasing
18 Death announcement
20 Healing plant
21 Letter stroke
22 Prior
23 Southern compass point
26 Acquire
28 Scottish one
29 Canadian group who sang "Steal My Sunshine"
31 Climbed
33 Finale
34 Sympathetic expression
35 View again
37 Short debutante

39 Profit per single stock
40 Goodyear balloon
43 Aviation abbreviation
45 Holy table
46 Build
50 Anger
51 Decorate a present
52 Tall plant
53 Nada
54 Having sufficient power
55 Logical operator
56 Young lady

1 Reverses
2 A road
3 Wing flaps
4 Shakespearean night
5 Defeat
6 Elder
7 Tropical edible plant
8 Zodiac ram

9 Fountain or ballpoint
10 Droop
13 Student
17 Fermented beverage
19 Liberal (abbr.)
22 Freshwater fish
24 Outlaw
25 Marry
27 Dulles or La Guardia
29 A youth
30 Female sheep
32 Arguer
33 Modifying
36 Every
38 Trite
39 Emergency Response Team
41 Santa ___
42 Shampoo brand
44 Glimpse
46 Civil Works Administration
47 Globe
48 Vase
49 Chairman of the board

Chapter Eight

Not Just a Puzzle

The creation of something new is not accomplished by the intellect but by the play instinct acting from inner necessity. The creative mind plays with the objects it loves.

—Carl Jung

The artistic expression in crossword puzzles is not just relegated to the constructor. Many others have found ways to express their love and appreciation of crosswords through other outlets—marriage proposals, invitations, novels, poetry, paintings, and Web blogs. As the years have progressed, crosswords have found their way on to many objects. A search for "crossword puzzles" on eBay led to results with images on T-shirts, greeting cards, coffee mugs, bracelet charms, fabric, and rubber stamps. The craze has swept the nation and appears to be here to stay.

Artistic Zen

Laurence G. Boldt, in *Zen and the Art of Making a Living*, talks of four ways to recognize a work of art. The first way is that the work of art is inspired, the second that the work of art is useful, the third that the work of art is natural, and the fourth is that the work of art is beautiful. In following these, it's easy to see the Zen philosophy applied to artistic uses and attempts. If the art is inspired, it is conceived through some connection to a higher spirit through your heightened senses. If the piece is useful to mankind, whether it directly assists in daily tasks or speaks to the senses and allows a moment of reflection, it speaks to the unity of everyone and a goal of bettering the universe. If the art is natural, it is created with ease; it is not forced or contrived. It comes from a strong sense of self and an artist who is well centered. If the final work is beautiful, it is as perfect as the creator could obtain. It is made with the best intentions, and even the imperfections contain character and work to make the art an extension of the artist.

Boldt wrote that, "Zen and art can teach us how to work beautifully . . . From art we can draw lessons—the lessons of the spirit at work (the inspiration of the artist) and the lessons of education to and sacrifice for the vision one sees. Zen says: No sense waiting for Heaven."

Common Wedding Phrase (1,2)

How would you feel if you were solving a crossword puzzle, only to find that the solutions were turning into clues themselves— clues to a question that your fiancé was getting ready to ask? That's just what happened in January 1998 to Emily Mindel. Her fiancé Bill Gottlieb used the *New York Times* crossword puzzle to indicate his intentions, ultimately using 56 Across to ask the question "Will you marry me?" for him.

Bill solicited the help of Will Shortz to help in his proposal. Will agreed and created the personalized puzzle, strategically placing clues that would provide their first names and other wedding topics in the solutions.

The story was reported in multiple newspapers and the articles say that Emily worked out the puzzle over brunch at a restaurant. Bill sat across from her and pretended to read his newspaper. A quarter of the way through the puzzle Emily knew something was up, although Bill still feigned indifference. When the puzzle was almost complete, he kissed her and asked her to marry him. Emily said yes.

Other crossword fans have followed suit and even though this method of proposing has grown in popularity, the recipients are still caught off guard as they uncover the solutions. Lee Glickstein, founder of Speaking Circles International in San Anselmo, California, told me of the proposal he made to his wife, Audrey Seymour. It was about two years ago, and he constructed a crossword puzzle that Will helped to edit. "I have a relationship with Will Shortz (though I have never met him) since he has edited and published several of my daily and Sunday crosswords," Lee said. "So he was delighted to edit the clues and point out some problems and make some suggestions." The puzzle was not published, but Lee disguised it as a Monday *New York Times* puzzle, and he printed it out using a software program. "Audrey at the time was only doing Monday puzzles, and we'd do them together in the evening. So she thought this was just another one. Quite a surprise to discover the message!" Lee was able to conceal his identity as author of the puzzle by anagramming his name to be "Ken Stegicelli" as the constructor.

Lee was kind enough to send me the puzzle to view, and I discovered the following clues, signifying his proposal:

Clue 17 Across: "Beginning of a personal message"
Solution: TOAUDREYFROMLEE
Clue 41 Across: "Middle of the message"
Solution: AQUESTIONARISES
Clue 67 Across: "End of the message"
Solution: WILLYOUBEMYWIFE
Clue 74 Across: "Happy ending beginning words"
Solution: IDO

Audrey shared her side of the story. "It was a Monday night," she related. "That's easy to remember because at the time, Monday night puzzles were the only *New York Times* crossword puzzles that I could solve on my own. I was beginning to share Lee's love of crossword puzzles, which wasn't hard because I had always loved puzzles in general. Often we would curl up together at the end of the day, each with our own puzzle or two."

So, like many Monday nights, Audrey asked Lee to print out the *New York Times* puzzle. "We plumped up the pillows, invited the cats to join us, and set to work—me with my typical beginner's puzzle, and he with whatever advanced puzzles he downloaded from the Internet."

In those days, Audrey said she would leave the theme until last, since she considered the long entries the hardest. "This one was a routine puzzle—but then about a third of the way through, suddenly the letters "TOAUD" sprang out at me—in the first line of a quote that was clued "Beginning of a personal message." I went cold and then hot all at once because I knew what it must be. Not wanting to make a fool of myself by jumping to conclusions, I kept quiet while feeling I was swimming in a whirlpool. I stole a glance over at Lee as best I could without turning my head, and he was just penning away with no outer sign of anything unusual. Darn, no help there!"

Audrey continued solving the puzzle, filling in more and more of the grid. As her suspicions proved to be true, she decided to slow down and take an extraordinary amount of time in solving it, just to keep the suspense going for Lee. "Finally, I couldn't stand it any longer and said 'Do I have to write a puzzle to respond?' Luckily he said no. But, I made him wait until I finished every last square before giving my answer. My answer was yes."

Happy _____ to You (8 Letters)

It's not only proposals that make for great crossword themes. Party invitations, anniversaries, graduations, and other life occasions make for great fodder as well. Keith Engers from Cape Town, South Africa, composed a crossword puzzle as an invitation to his forty-fifth birthday party. "It was what Dell crosswords call an

Anacrostic—where you solve the clues and transfer the letters to a diagram to reveal a quotation," he said. "Every invitation I sent out was responded to, but one or two friends said they had almost tossed it away, thinking it was an advertising gimmick for some unwanted product."

Crossword Plots

One day I was conducting research on crossword puzzles and art when I stumbled across a Web site for *The Crossword Mystery* series, a set of novels by Nero Blanc. In reading through the Web site I learned that Nero Blanc is actually the pen name for the writing duo Steve Zettler and Cordelia Frances Biddle. The Web site further explained that they came up with the name Nero Blanc as their pseudonym because nero is the Italian word for black, and blanc is the French word for white. They refuse to say, and there's no way of immediately guessing, which term refers to which of their personalities.

I sent the pair an e-mail in the hopes of speaking with them about the book series, figuring it would be a good fit with the artistic use of crossword puzzles. Within minutes, I received a reply suggesting that we speak the next morning.

The next morning I was up bright an early, getting the girls out of bed and out of my hair. I settled down in my office with a cup of coffee and the phone for my 8:00 interview. (It was 11:00 where they live in the heart of Philadelphia.)

Steve quickly picked up the phone, and his warm, quiet voice assured me that the couple needed a break from writing and was inviting the distraction of the interview. He was working on a new crossword puzzle for an upcoming novel and was stuck on one of the diagonal entries.

He signaled for Cordelia to get on her phone. (I'm assuming in her office upstairs. Cordelia told me that they work in offices on different floors. Steve was downstairs, because "we can't possibly work in the same room," she explained.) Her energetic, upbeat tone set the pace for our conversation. After a quick introduction and a discussion of the merits of living on the west coast—they had previously lived in Los Angeles, and I once resided in Manhattan—we were ready to discuss their series.

Between the two of them, Steve and Cordelia gave me a primer to the characters in the books. Belle Graham is a crossword editor who dislikes the nickname "Anagram" (constructed by using her first name Anabelle and her last name) and chooses to go by Belle to avoid any further antagonizing. Rosco Polycrates is a private investigator who meets up with Belle in the first novel while he is investigating the murder of a flamboyant crossword editor. Rosco approaches Belle, a local competitor to the murder victim, to learn more about the industry. This interaction leads to the two working to solve the mystery, successfully, which further leads to more mysteries and their eventual marriage. Each of the books within the series contains six unique crossword puzzles integrated within the plot. The reader is able to solve the puzzles along with Rosco and Belle. The crossword puzzles are typically sent in to the main characters, or found, as clues to a murder. Each novel combines the traditional whodunit with the added mystery of determining which individual in the book is creating and distributing the crossword puzzles.

Cordelia informs me that the idea for the series came one day when the pair sat over their daily crossword puzzle at lunch. Steve and Cordelia originally met while working as actors in New York years ago. They moved on to writing and are both published under their own names, Cordelia focusing primarily on historical fiction while Steve pens international thrillers. They found that writing kept them apart, something they were not used to after their years on the stage. The only problem was that they found it difficult to discuss their individual novels with one another. Steve said, "as writers we missed working together and we were searching for something to put our heads together." They decided to integrate crossword puzzles into their daily routine, as a way to unwind and spend time with each other. One day Cordelia became frustrated with the current puzzle and said, "someone should just kill this guy!" A light bulb went off. They quickly decided to create a murder mystery based on someone killing off a crossword puzzle editor.

Both Steve and Cordelia thought the project would be fun and a way to collaborate together, something they had been contemplating for a while. They liked the idea of a murder mystery because it wasn't as dark and heavy as the genres of writing that they typically focus on individually. Nero Blanc evolved as their pen name for the series.

"We both write with very different styles. Nero Blanc is just another person who lives in this house," Cordelia said. "Steve does the crossword puzzles. I am hopeless. I come up with a possible solution but then find that I need two more squares to make it work."

I asked Steve if he uses computer software to create the puzzles, and he quickly said no, for two reasons. The first is that he uses a Mac and the software doesn't run on that operating system, a dilemma I've had to overcome as well. The second is that the crosswords that they incorporate into the novels contain many of the character's names and specific clues to the mystery, so he finds that he is better off creating the puzzle by hand. Steve sits down with graph paper and a pencil and sketches out each 15 × 15 puzzle. In the first book, they purposely created each character with fifteen characters in their full names. For this reason, Rosco's name does not have an "e" at the end. Roscoe Polycrates would have had sixteen letters, whereas Rosco Polycrates only has fifteen. All of the names have hidden names and word play, making the characters themselves part of the crossword collection. In one of their later novels, *Anatomy of a Crossword*, each of the names of the characters are anagrams for famous people in the movie industry.

Steve and Cordelia are very aware that their writing styles are diverse. They have come up with a unique system for writing the novels. If a chapter is predominantly about Rosco and his views, Steve begins the initial authoring. The same is true for Belle and Cordelia. When Steve finishes a chapter, he swaps the piece and Cordelia rewrites it, adding her own writing style and conversation pieces. "We always up the ante and trade back and forth, sometimes up to four times," Cordelia said. "It's like play-ing a game."

I was curious to know if Nero Blanc gets feedback about the books themselves. Cordelia responds in the affirmative. One person wrote in to thank the authors. Never much of a reader, the fan had picked up one of the novels due to a love of cross-word puzzles and now enjoys reading. Of course not all of the feedback is positive. Steve was quick to jump in and say, "Cross-word buffs are on top of the puzzles." In one puzzle he wrote in "Canadian Province" as the clue to the solution YUKON. He later discovered that Yukon is a Canadian territory, not a province, and he got a few unhappy readers writing in. It is amusing to the couple that they've come full circle and now have readers want-ing to "murder them" for their puzzles.

The duo still solves a crossword each day. Cordelia said, "At lunch we plop down a puzzle in between us." She insists upon holding the pen (they only solve a puzzle in ink) although the pair discusses each clue before inking it in. Often one of them will get the answer where the other one doesn't. "It's how your brain works; you get that little pun or that one letter, " Cordelia said. They shred their crossword puzzles after solving them. They don't want anyone getting ahold of a puzzle that might contain mistakes, seeing as how they write about crosswords. Cordelia mentioned to me that someone once told her that solving a cross-word is like solving a linear problem. It uses progression, which she later equated to writing murder mysteries. You go from clue to clue to come up with the final solution.

The couple insists upon sharing their good fortune with others and donates a portion of their earnings from the Nero Blanc books. They recently auctioned off of one of the names of a character in an upcoming novel, donating the winnings to the Alzheimer's Foundation.

Poetry in Crossword Motion

Have you ever looked at a crossword puzzle and found the list of clues to be poetic, humorous, or interesting in their own right? Peter Valentine certainly thinks so. I caught up with him one day as he was running to an appointment in a torrential downpour in New York City, where he lives. I was luckily ensconced in my office in San Diego, the warm air and clear skies a stark contrast to the weather he was experiencing. This was just one of several of phone conversations that we had, resulting from an e-mail I sent Peter earlier in the week. I contacted him regarding his crossword related poetry, something I found browsing through the posts at the *New York Times*, "Today's Puzzle" forum.

Peter writes poems based on the *New York Times* crossword puzzle and publishes it on his Web site—*www.hungrybutscared .com*. He has been doing this since April 2002 and has now written more than 500 poems. Each poem has the same structure. The first stanza is created using only the words contained within the Across clues. The second stanza is created only using the words contained within the Down clues. The third stanza is created only using answers within the grid. The title of the poem can contain words from any part of the puzzle. Peter is very strict about not using any words in his poem that didn't appear in the puzzle. Peter said. "If the number one appears, I can use it as the letter I." If the word "the" is not anywhere in the clues or solution, then the word "the" cannot appear in the poem. He does, however, give himself some flexibility when it comes to punctuation and repetition of any of the words.

I asked Peter how he first came up with the idea for writing poetry based on crossword puzzles. "This is how I began the project, sitting one morning, blowing off work, and mulling over a tough Thursday puzzle," he replied. "At a certain point, I stopped trying to figure out the answer to a clue and just let my eyes wander from word to word and my thoughts to their associations. Then I wrote a poem." He thought it was a fun idea, kind of cool, and decided he should do it for a week. After the first poem, which was much more freeform than the current works, he created a better, stricter format.

After a week of creating poems, Peter continued writing, with the goal of doing it indefinitely. For four or five months, he worked religiously creating the poems, but then, according to Peter, life got crazy. Around his one-year anniversary of the project, he wrote his last poem. Or so he thought. Six months later he took it up again because he enjoyed the writing and wanted to continue, and he now sends out some of his "better" poems to people who sign up on his e-mail list through the Web site or by contacting him directly. Although he publishes all poems on the Web site, he chooses only his favorites to distribute through e-mail.

Peter tries to publish the poem the same day that a puzzle comes out (he only writes from crosswords printed in the *New York Times*), and so he works his way through the crossword each day, completing the puzzle himself. It takes him approximately forty-five minutes to do both—solve the puzzle and write the poem. He used to focus on creating great poems, but recently took the pressure off himself. He said that he thinks the poems actually got better without the additional restraint.

"Due to the strict rules of the poem, I am forced to explore the relations that every word has with any other, turn words on their heads, juxtapose words that rarely meet," Peter said. Through this process, he finds meaning in places where previously only a game existed. "For the crossword puzzle enthusiast mulling over word clues, the thoughts that do not lead to solutions are discarded. Modern day life requires much the same. The rigors of society compel people to focus narrowly on solving problems that lead to prescribed and limited results. Any attention paid to the incidental ideas that cross or conflict may be time lost. My poem pays attention to the incidental ideas."

Peter said that his poems address the need for people to pay attention to the incidental ideas. "My readers enjoy the daily availability of my poem," he went on to say. "The work is accessible and often fun. In the dialogue of poetry, my daily poem says, 'Poetry can be found anywhere you take the time to look.'"

I asked Peter if he has any favorite poems. He mentioned that he has written several based on his father (who he solves crossword puzzles with during family get-togethers) and his son.

"There is one that is sort of descriptive of what I do. It's from early March, and it's called 'i deal in words.'"

03/04/2005

i deal in words

across
i work quickly, fill in words
plant fruit in words when i can
some pregnant words mixed with words to grow anew
like lovers, words
whisperers

like...

down
in the sudden tongue of "windmill"
the inspiration of arm, feather, violence

and...

answers
    the life-force
in "gasp"

Puzzling Times

One day I Googled the term "crossword puzzles paintings," and I stumbled upon the piece *Puzzling Times*, an oil painting by photorealist, Steve Mills. I looked at the painting online and got the sensation that I was most certainly looking at a photograph, not a painting. The image is gorgeous, the shadows are perfect, and you want to reach into the scene and begin solving the puzzle. The piece measures 46 × 60 inches and depicts the March 23, 2003, edition of the *New York Times*. The publication is lying open to the crossword puzzle, with "The Arts" section just visible underneath the folded paper. The puzzle is slightly obscured by a pen and pencil, a beat-up crossword dictionary, and a magnifying glass.

I immediately e-mailed Steve to see if he was willing to talk about the painting, and he encouraged me to give him a call. Not too early though, as he stays up late at night and sleeps in late in the morning. This works perfect for me, as he is three time zones ahead of me in Florida.

I called Steve later in the week. He picked up the phone in his gallery and pleasantly responded to the interview. I explained about the book and how I found *Puzzling Times*. Steve proceeded to tell me that it is just one of a series of paintings he has created for the Granary Gallery in Martha's Vineyard. He is currently working to complete a new painting for the series consisting of a baseball sitting on top of the front page of the Boston Globe with the headline "At Last" dating to when the Red Sox won the World Series. Steve does a lot of work with still life, with many of his pieces including marbles or game pieces.

"The idea came together because of the ratty old crossword dictionary. It was one of the employees' mother's crossword books," he said, speaking of an employee at the Granary Gallery. He worked with them to come up with ideas for the series of paintings. After an initial brainstorming, they solidified the ideas and work out some photos of the props. For this painting, Steve just grabbed a Sunday edition of the newspaper, which happened to have a crossword puzzle contributed by Con Pederson and an acrostic puzzle by Cox & Rathvon. Steve confirms that every clue and clue number, even the article below the puzzle, are perfectly legible. He did replace one clue with his wife's name, saying "I like to put her name or initials in paintings. They are usually very tiny, and it takes some time to find them." The remainder of the clues are the same as the original puzzle.

Steve spent 333 hours on the painting (he only paints one at a time) completing it on July 20, 2003. He keeps a precise log in a database he started twenty-five years ago. "It's really paid off!" he said after I ask him about the length of time it took to finish the project, and he quickly looked it up. This painting sold for $60,000 to a law firm on Park Avenue in New York City.

"A funny story about this painting. Here it is hanging in the gallery, when the actual author of the crossword puzzle stumbled in and saw it. He was with his wife. I was in the gallery that day, and they were so excited about the painting," Steve said. "I was getting referrals from all over the place."

Blogging It

With the plethora of Weblogs (blogs) that have arisen on the Internet in the past few years, it's no surprise that people are now journaling about their crossword expeditions. Blogs are online journals where people rant, rave, talk, quote, post pictures, and otherwise keep a diary on one subject or another. You'll find blogs on politics, parenting, career choices, hobbies, and much more. I jumped on the blog bandwagon over a year ago with my personal blog that discusses parenting and writing. I created a second blog recently—a stamping blog that discusses rubber-stamping on cards and scrapbook pages. I include gallery items, techniques, card templates, and news on new stamps. It's a great addition to the actual stamping, one of my favorite hobbies, and a way for me to share my layouts and techniques with the world.

Debra Hamel, a writer and ancient historian from North Haven, Connecticut, started *the-deblog.blogspot.com* (one of multiple Weblogs that she maintains) in June 2004. With this blog, she was looking for a place to document general observations and commentary, something she was working to avoid on her book review blog, *www.book-blog.blogspot.com.* By her fourth post (as determined by her archives) Debra was already talking about crossword puzzles and how she had finished the *New York Times* puzzle (a Monday one) in about ten minutes. I asked Debra what made her write about crosswords. "Shortly before I started the-deblog.com I began trying to train myself so I could complete crosswords," she responded. "Prior to that I just hadn't done them much, and when I had tried I'd found them very difficult. Of course, after you do them for a while you start thinking the right way, leaping to the secondary meanings a phrase might have, for example. So I got a bit better at them. And during all this, pretty much right away, I started blogging about my attempts to do the *New York Times* puzzles."

It didn't take Debra long before she was discussing the various clues and puzzles on her blog, and by August 2004, she was placing the answers in the comments section of her posts regarding the theme-related clues in the Sunday puzzles. "Apart from it being fun for me, and something to blog about, I found that a surprisingly large number of people go hunting on a Sunday for crossword answers," Debra said. "It brings in a fair amount of traffic to the blog, so I figure it behooves me to keep it up."

Debra still continues to solve multiple crosswords throughout the week. She tries to complete the Monday through Thursday puzzles and always tackles the Sunday ones so she can document it on her Web site. She even constructed a crossword puzzle of her own for a contest she held on the blog. The puzzle was vaguely related to the classics, and the winner won an autographed copy of her book, *Trying Neaira: The True Story of a Courtesan's Scandalous Life in Ancient Greece*.

We Are All Artists

Everyone is an artist. Perhaps not in the traditional sense of painters and musicians, poets and authors, but each of us has something to contribute creatively to the universe. A passage in *The Zen of Creativity*, by John Daido Loori, sums it up perfectly:

> *Zen, and by extension the Zen aesthetic, shows us that all things are perfect and complete just as they are. Nothing is lacking. In trying to realize our true nature, we rub against the same paradox: We don't know that we already are what we are trying to become . . . Each one of us is already an artist, whether we realize it or not. In fact, it doesn't matter whether we realize it—this truth of perfection is still there. Engaging the creative process is a way of getting in touch with this truth, and to let it function in all areas of our lives.*

Try This

Take a crossword puzzle and construct a poem out of it. You can use any framework you want, even turning words around and making amusing layouts. If you happen to use the structure outlined by Peter Valentine, feel free to submit your poem to him for consideration (e-mail him at *pbvalentine@earthlink.net*). He may just place it on his Web site and earn you your five minutes of fame!

Just for fun, I created this poem from the crossword puzzle that appeared in the *New York Times* on my birthday:

05/06/2005

ancient you

across
it's only hard commuting
occupational
don't just stand there
towed vehicle, maybe

down
like some of the high points
end of vacation
a little stunt
oh no

answers
grenade district
a game
what am I?
a la mode

The Act of Manipulation

1 Obtain
4 Hertz
7 Petty fight
11 Sunglasses protect eyes from this
12 Painting, literature, and more
14 Memo
15 Hawaiian necklace
16 Roman emperor
17 Eternity
18 Competitive offer
20 Mischievous elf
21 Put into place
23 Truant
26 Expert
27 Here and ___
30 Wine storage space
33 Colorless gas
35 Southern compass point
36 Tramp
38 Desired wine condition
39 Dismissal

42 Unit of pressure
44 Artistic decoration
48 Beers
49 Reverse
50 Dead ___ Scrolls
51 Tuft of hair
52 Sow
53 Fall behind
54 Lawyer (abbr.)
55 Bambi's mother
56 Before, poetically

1 Hurried swallow
2 Happily ___ after
3 More than a duo
4 Cathedral's clergyman
5 Printing machine
6 Earth layers
7 Escargot
8 Haiku, for one
9 At the top
10 First double digit
13 Console
19 Medicine tablet
22 Lease

23 American Cancer Society (abbr.)
24 Network of Deceit
25 Grand ___ Opry
27 Bother
28 Single
29 Marry
31 Lincoln's nickname
32 Commotion
34 Policeman's cry
37 Complained
39 Dangerous business
40 Tape
41 One electrode
42 Scheme
43 Faction
45 Island
46 Not far
47 Measuring device
48 Latin wing

Chapter Nine
They Won't Bite

Nothing comes from nothing.

—William Shakespeare

Crossword puzzles won't bite, or at least that's what I tell people who view the grids as the antipole of a good time. Not only will they not hurt you, they actually can assist in making you a healthier person. Studies show that solving crossword puzzles, along with other brain boosting and physical activities, can help ward off dementia and Alzheimer's disease. They also work in a multitude of ways to keep brains and fingers busy—assisting addicts in their quest to fight against their dependencies, helping retirees to keep busy and work their tired minds, and giving teachers tools to help their students remain alert and having fun.

A Slow Start

When crosswords began to sweep America off its collective puzzled feet in the 1920s, the puzzles were often seen in a negative light. Some people criticized the crosswords as being merely trivia. Managers blamed the puzzles as distractions and even went so far as to say they caused a lack of production among workers. At one point, the tiny black squares were accused of straining the eyes, although they were quickly exonerated.

On the other hand, as far back as the 1920s, researchers touted crosswords as having positive effects on one's health due to its stimulation of the brain. Today the research continues, and the results are even more encouraging than previously thought. Study after study shows that using the brain regularly, with activities like crossword puzzles, is a benefit in aging.

Lovatts Crosswords & Puzzles conducted an interview with Dr. George Singer, retired head of La Trobe University's School of Psychology, in April 1999. In the interview, Dr. Singer said that crosswords are an excellent tool for keeping the mind active, even better than chess and bridge because they involve the side of the brain concerned with language. Mental exercise is essential to keep the brain active and healthy, and exercising the mind impacts a person's health and how long they'll live. Dr. Singer went on to say, "We know that mental activity releases certain hormones. Some of these are important to immune functioning. Studies showed that crosswords caused the immune system to produce antibodies that helped people resist illness."

Refocus Your Mind

The National Cancer Institute offers information on managing radiation therapy in their *Guide to Self-Help During Cancer Treatment*. Many patients become nauseous and queasy prior to the cancer treatments because of their anxiety and concerns. The institute suggests finding a way to relieve tension before the radiation therapy by refocusing your mind on something other than the upcoming procedure. The say "reading a book, writing a letter, or working a crossword puzzle may help you relax." These same activities are also recommended for patients who experience nausea and vomiting after chemotherapy.

Curb Addictions

Many articles and institutions, including the American Lung Association, tout the benefits of crossword puzzles as a way to distract someone from a cigarette craving. They suggest solving a crossword puzzle to keep your mind and hands busy when the urge to smoke sneaks up. Other ideas include knitting, taking a shower, doodling, crocheting, and playing solitaire. The American Heart Association recommends reaching for a crossword puzzle instead of a snack, which is what many smokers do in their attempt to break the habit. Crossword puzzles help to prevent adding on pounds while quitting smoking.

My mother, Barb Lauritzen, started smoking at the age of fourteen. When she turned fifty, for a multitude of reasons, including a new granddaughter on the way, she decided to quit smoking by using the patch. As anyone with an addiction knows, while breaking that habit it is important to keep busy, both physically and mentally. Barb took up latch-hooking rugs during her free time—something her father had done for years. "He told me it was very soothing to just put yourself into a 'zone' to keep your mind off other things. He was right." The latch-hooking helped to keep her fingers busy, but looking back she wishes she had also occupied her mind using crosswords or some other form of puzzles. Three years after her journey to quit smoking, she currently subscribes to *GAMES* magazine and uses the puzzles as a stress reliever and to continue to fight any rare urges to smoke.

Prevent Alzheimer's

The Buddha wrote, "We do not learn by experience, but by our capacity for experience," and seemed to anticipate current thinking on Alzheimer's.

In 2001, Dr. Robert Friedland, a neurologist at Case Western Reserve University School of Medicine in Cleveland, led a groundbreaking study on Alzheimer's disease. The study combined mental, physical, and social activities in adults, and compared those activity levels with the rate of development of Alzheimer's disease. The results were published in the *Proceedings of the National Academy of Sciences*, and the study showed that it is never too late to start building your brain muscle. Dr. Amir Soas, a coinvestigator in the study, advised Baby Boomers who want to lower their risks of developing Alzheimer's disease to read, solve crossword puzzles, or learn a new hobby—anything that would help to engage the mind. He also suggested steering clear of the television, as that activity allows your brain to idle in neutral.

Claudia Tropila, an attorney from Fountain Valley, California, agrees with Dr. Soas. She attributes much of the upswing in Alzheimer's cases to "the TV generation getting old. Fewer readers and less mind stimulation. Radio is much better."

Gordon Murray from St. Helens, Merseyside, said that the use of crossword puzzles to ward off dementia and Alzheimer's is a subject that greatly interests him. "My mother died a couple of years ago after a long struggle with Alzheimer's," he explains. "I've been a crossword addict since the age of five, so will Alzheimer's affect me? According to my wife it already has! But that's only because I get so involved with apparently intractable clues that I forget about 'reality' and what I really ought to be doing."

Study findings on activity and Alzheimer's were released in 2003. The research was published in the *New England Journal of Medicine,* and it showed that crossword puzzles did indeed have a direct affect on lessening the impacts of Alzheimer's disease. The study, *Leisure Activities and the Risk of Dementia in the Elderly*, was conducted over a twenty-one-year period at the Albert Einstein College of Medicine of Yeshiva University, New York. Dr. Joe Verghese, assistant professor of neurology, led the program. The team monitored a group of 469 men and women over the age of seventy-five who were not already suffering from dementia. Each participant gave details on how often they participated in various cognitive activities (including crossword puzzles) and physical activities.

While there was no significant association between the physical activities, except dancing, and a reduced risk of dementia, the results did find that people who took part in intellectually stimulating activities had a reduced risk of contracting the symptoms. The depreciation was directly correlated to the frequency of participation in the activity of choice. When using their models and crossword puzzles as an example, an elderly person who solved crossword puzzles four times a week had a 47 percent lower risk of contracting dementia than a subject who solved puzzles once a week. The findings further strengthened those who believe in the "use it or lose it" theory of continuing to mentally stimulate your brain to preserve memory and mental sharpness as you age.

David Gamon and Allen D. Bragdon wrote in their book, *Building Mental Muscle*, that researchers have evidence that physical and mental exercise can double the rate at which new brain cells are created from the neural stem cells. "This sort of mechanism may be at play in the studies that indicate a self-challenging lifestyle may have a preventive effect against Alzheimer's." The book also contains information on the way your six zones of practical intelligence operate (executive planning & social interaction, memory, emotional response, language, math, and creative special visualization). You'll find exercises designed to stimulate the cells in each brain zone, a few of which you may not regularly use in your daily and professional life. Along with the text and graphics, they've included mind games, memory tests, and crossword puzzles to quiz you and teach you how to use your brain effectively.

Giving us further evidence, Ian Williams from Canberra, Australia, said that his father died at eighty-eight "fully compos mentis," and he completed the majority of a quick crossword most days.

The Alzheimer's Association publishes a pamphlet called "Maintain your Brain." On the first page they provide a list of "Ten Ways to Maintain Your Brain." I was pleased to discover that number six, Jog Your Mind, suggests keeping your brain active and engaged to increase its vitality and build reserves of brain cells and connections. "Read, write, play games, do crossword puzzles," it suggests. In the "Mental Activity" section, the pamphlet tells you that an altered connection among brain cells results in a mental decline as you age. Fortunately research has found that working the brain appears to build its vitality and may work to build reserves of brain cells and connections. "You don't have to turn your life upside down or make extreme changes to achieve many of these benefits," the pamphlet suggests. "Start with something small, like a walk. After a while, add another small change." They also advocate a brain-healthy diet, exercise, and social activity, along with a crossword puzzle here and there.

There are some who are still skeptical of the findings, and others who have family members who solved crossword puzzles religiously, only to find them battling Alzheimer's disease as they aged. Luckily, there are no known health risks associated with crossword puzzles, so it won't hurt those of us who choose to partake in the activity.

The Other Senses

Although crossword puzzles are a great way to work the brain, and a healthy pastime to integrate into your daily routine, a type of mental exercise called neurobics encourages using all of your senses, in unusual ways, to help exercise your mind. The term neurobics was developed by Dr. Lawrence C. Katz, a neurobiology professor at Duke University, and writer Manning Rubin. Together they authored the book *Keep Your Brain Alive*, containing eighty-three exercises that help increase mental fitness and help to prevent memory loss.

The book proposes doing a variety of activities during the day that will stimulate your senses and use them in unusual ways. The goal is to keep the senses guessing. One of the exercises suggest brushing your teeth with the opposite hand than you normally do, while another urges you to try sniffing vanilla first thing in the morning. Perhaps you'd rather attempt to unlock your door with your eyes closed or drive with mittens on your hands? According to Dr. Katz, these neurboics starts the flow of neurotrophins or growth-promoting molecules. These neurotrophins create new circuits that assist in improving your memory, creativity, and logical thinking.

Neurobics isn't touted as a way to develop a super brain or a method to remember the names of people you meet at a party. Instead they are exercises to assist you in growing and processing information on the different pathways that crisscross your brain. You can do them at any time, or during any activity. Just try changing seats at the dinner table or wear earplugs when you watch television. Or the next time you solve a crossword puzzle, do it while standing up—or try turning on the radio and listening to a station you've never tuned into before.

Teaching Tools

I personally find crossword puzzles to be a great educational tool. If I don't know a solution, I look it up. I then do my best to retain that knowledge for the next crossword puzzle, trivia game, or social situation where it might be of some use. I couldn't remember that Charles Darwin wrote a book entitled *The Origin of Species* until I had to use the title in a crossword puzzle solution, but you can be sure that I won't forget it again.

If crossword puzzles help to teach me current events and historical facts, what use could they be in a school setting? Some linguistics experts say that puzzles have educational value, as well as acting as a diversion or relaxation device. An article in the November 2000 edition of the University of California's *Daily Bruin* contains an interview with Ed Stabler, a linguistics professor. He related his work on computational linguistics to crossword puzzles, saying the way computer programs solve crossword puzzles is similar to how we understand language.

To clarify his comment, he uses an example of when you listen to someone speak in a crowded atmosphere. If a noise overlaps what they are saying, you can typically fill in the gaps based on the conversation and context of the words that you do hear. Crossword puzzles are similar because they require the solver to fill in the gaps of a word, using the context of the clues and the surrounding letters within the grid.

Crossword puzzles can provide an education to anyone who pays attention to the solutions they are uncovering. Roots of words, including Latin roots, pop up in many of the solutions. You are also forced to build your vocabulary; not many people who don't do crosswords know that the definition of "excelsior" is higher, for example. I've even found myself learning about classic literature and retaining bits of artistic information like Wassily Kandinsky painted *The Blue Mountain*. Crossword puzzles are even used to help reinforce Braille teachings to blind students, using a plastic board with Braille letter tiles.

Kathi Regalbuto, a mother from Summerville, North Carolina who homeschools and owns Positive Results for Homeschoolers LLC, said she used puzzles extensively in teaching her daughter spelling. Her daughter "was of the opinion that spelling correctly was irrelevant and close enough was fine," she said. "She wanted to do crossword puzzles because she had seen me doing them, but of course transposing, adding, or omitting letters in a crossword puzzle just does not work."

I posed the question to Gretchen, another mother who homeschools, and she thought incorporating crosswords into her curriculum was a great idea. "We've always just used them for fun activities that subtly encourage fluency and proficiency in the concepts we study, but you could also use them as a form of testing," she pondered. "In multiple choice you get a list of answers to choose from; whereas if you designed a test in a crossword format, you would have to know and visualize the proper word without having it spelled out for you. Anyone can play the letter game with multiple choice, but this sort of evaluation is more fun while it requires greater proficiency with the subject matter to complete properly. And if done correctly, it even serves as a self-checking mechanism for knowledge."

Helen Donahue, a Life Maskmaker and homeschool teacher from Eastern North Carolina told me, "When I began home-schooling my grandson (in sixth grade at the time), he was having a difficult time with spelling/vocabulary." Helen kept a list of weekly spelling words and definitions that her grandson missed during the month. She would use that list to construct a cross-word puzzle, and then have him work on it during the weekend. "If he'd ask about the spelling of a word, I'd tell him to look it up in the dictionary. It did seem sort of 'crazy' to look up a word you don't know how to spell, but believe me . . . it does work. We did the puzzles every Friday. Now that he is in high school, we buy puzzle and logic books to work on. These are done, usually, during the weekends and holidays."

Helen said she'd never forget the first time her grandson asked about the spelling of a word because it just didn't fit in the boxes of the puzzle. "I tried everything I could to get him to sound it out and spell it correctly. After several minutes of working with him, failed attempts, and getting frustrated, I handed him Webster's dictionary and told him to 'look it up'! He looked at me in total shock and asked how he was supposed to find the correct spelling and definition in the dictionary if he didn't know how to spell it to begin with. I told him to 'just use your brain and do it.' It took him a while, but he learned very quickly how to properly sound out his words, use the power of elimination, and find them in the dictionary. To this day he might begin to ask what a word means, but will very quickly say 'never mind, I'll find it myself' and grab the dictionary. The coolest thing now is . . . he'll find words that I have never heard of and quiz me on them. If I don't know the spelling or definition, he'll look at me and say, "Look it up in the dictionary!"

Learning English

In the teaching of English as a second language, crossword puzzles can be incorporated to reinforce vocabulary and thematic lessons. In an article for *ESL Magazine*, Christine Meloni wrote, "A fun way to study vocabulary in a foreign language is to do crossword puzzles. For this reason, the editors of the Internet TESL Journal launched the 'Crossword Puzzles for ESL Students' project." The project now contains many crossword puzzles, categorized by their level of ability. The themes of the crossword puzzles cover everything from animals, foods, and body parts—to parts of speech and verb tenses. Other ESL Web sites have incorporated crossword puzzles into their curriculum, while also offering them to the educational community at large. In my searches, I found crossword puzzles on the topics of fruits, sports, chores, math, outer space, verbs, seasons, and more. These puzzles are smaller in nature, six to ten words, and only intersect the other crossword entries at one or two letters.

Mommy Relaxation

It wasn't long ago that my daughter was an infant. I can remember sitting on the floor of her pale green nursery, stifling a yawn as I leaned over to kiss her toes. She cooed and smiled and kicked her tiny feet. I grinned and said, "Mama loves your toesie woesies," and tickled them again. A moment later, the phone rang and I rushed to answer it. My husband was calling to let me know that he'd be home late for dinner. As I went to hang up the phone I barely stopped myself from saying the words "byesie wysie," an impulse that horrified me the remainder of the day.

In speaking to other moms at my playgroups, I learn that almost every mom has a story similar to mine. They are so used to speaking baby talk, reciting colors and body parts, that they find themselves using the same high-pitched voice and language with their spouses and friends. Because of this, we are all very eager to engage in adult conversation and find an outlet in these playgroups with each other and the other moms. We meet on a weekly basis at parks and each other's homes while our children work on their social interaction and sharing skills.

Of course, that only gets us so far. Our topics of conversation rarely extend further than the latest "baby signs" book or the best methods to soothe a teething toddler. One woman tells me that she recently felt very out of place while attending a happy hour event with her husband because she was not up on many of the current events. She found that she was very out of the loop with the latest news and Hollywood happenings. When she was conversing with her husband's colleagues and coworkers, her interesting stories and exclamations of her son's first steps fell on deaf ears.

So what's a mom to do? In the interviews that I conducted, I found that crossword puzzles are a great tool in offering a relaxing outlet and use of the brain for moms who stay home with their infants and toddlers. Debbie Doll from Prairie du Chien, Wisconsin, enjoys solving crosswords daily to make her "mommy brain" think. She even finds that the crossword puzzles teach her patience—a great skill in parenting small children.

Sue Jones lives in the outskirts of Philadelphia, Pennsylvania. She considers herself a housewife and solves the Azed crossword puzzle in *The Observer* in bed on Sunday mornings with her husband as their weekly ritual. They settle down with a cup of tea and the Chambers dictionary for assistance. Sue has to have a pencil in her hand, using the tool as her "thinking stick." Sue said that solving crossword puzzles is "more of a way to keep my brain from rusting than an escape from the daily routine, but there's certainly an element of that, too. If you're 'just a mum' it's certainly satisfying to prove to yourself that you can still think!"

The sentiment even extends back to the time when crossword puzzles were first introduced. In 1925 a Philadelphia housewife wrote to a newspaper saying "A woman who has small children and has to be in her home a great deal of the time needs something to make her use her mental facilities. Cross-wording is just the thing."

Other stay-at-home moms found that crossword puzzles offered a way to relax and wind down from a frantic day with their children. Jenna Jones, a stay-at-home mom with two sons, Branden and Xander, in Des Moines, Iowa, shared her personal experience in parenting and crossword puzzles.

"I started really doing them a lot when I was pregnant with Xander because it actually seemed to help alleviate the pain I was having with my kidneys," she said. "I would stay up until 4:00 in the morning going crazy with the crosswords. I think I completed four books in just a few months. I even took them in the car with me when I would go pick Brendan up from school. Although it didn't help with the pain, it did keep me busy enough that my mind was taken off of it. I also got to the point that I would scan very quickly through the questions and fill in all the ones I knew for several puzzles in a row. Then I would go back and fill in the ones that actually took a bit of thought. I also took them to the hospital when I was in labor."

Jenna does them only sporadically now, mostly when she has some free time and needs to relax a bit. "I can tune just about everything out when I am working on one," she explained. "I would say that it relaxes me more than anything."

Try This

Take a conscious look at how crossword puzzles can affect your physical and mental health. Perhaps you can use them as assistance in the process of stopping a harmful habit. Maybe you can incorporate them into your family time and expand your child's vocabulary and spelling skills. You can even purchase crossword books or create your own to include in a care package for your child at camp or a holiday present for an elderly relative. The benefits of crossword puzzles are waiting to be discovered by those who choose to solve them.

The Many Benefits

1 Head cover
5 Clay mask
8 Tooth holder
11 Lowest female voice
12 Sprinkler attachment
13 Wide kimono sash
14 Sneer
15 The baby
17 New mother affliction
19 Publicize dirty laundry
20 Study
23 First artificial satellite
27 Faint
29 Actor Affleck
30 Insult
32 Check
33 Wrist accessory
36 Briefcase
39 An Asian peninsula
41 Cool Slang
42 Presenile dementia

47 Electric generators
50 Small desktop button
51 Act nosey
52 The Loch ___ monster
53 Siamese
54 Sew a folded edge
55 American College of Physicians (abbr.)
56 Arrange

1 Placid
2 Margarine
3 Individual unit
4 Layout
5 Make secure
6 Customary
7 Contradicts
8 Brand ___ boxer
9 Six pack muscles
10 Mental ability
12 Composite
16 Chew
18 Female passive force

21 Reserve Officers Training Corps (abbr.)
22 Arc builder
23 South by west
24 Reach maximum level
25 Until
26 Sephia manufacturer
28 North by East
31 Afflict
34 Ocean Spray's drink starters
35 *A Midsummer Night's Dream* lover
37 Thai
38 Acknowledges
40 Ancient Mexican civilization
43 Hospital (abbr.)
44 Reverberate
45 Lion noise
46 Irritation
47 Automobile speed
48 Be
49 Place to exercise

Chapter Ten

The Future Is Now

Life can be found only in the present moment. The past is gone, the future is not yet here, and if we do not go back to ourselves in the present moment, we cannot be in touch with life.

—Thich Nhat Hanh

I t is estimated that more than 50 million Americans solve crossword puzzles occasionally, with more than 30 million of them solving at least one puzzle a month. That's an amazing amount of solvers, and the numbers grow even more significant when you look to the cryptic crosswords of Great Britain and other countries where crossword popularity is increasing. According to the Massachusetts Institute of Technology, crossword puzzles exist in every major alphabet-based language across the world. With so many fans looking to solve puzzles as their days progress, crossword puzzles now appear on the Internet, cellular phones, and have even entered the sportsmanship arena in the American Crossword Puzzle Tournament. Today's crossword puzzle fans aren't the solitary lot they used to be. Now they are outspoken and willing to share their commentary with their comrades and constructors at large.

Anyone Have a Mouse?

As with everything else, crossword puzzles have found their way onto the computer and Internet, and in a big way. New generations of puzzle solvers only know how to fill in the grid using a computer mouse. No pen-or-pencil dilemma for them. They don't even have to deal with newspaper ink or spilling food onto a newspaper or book. As for mistakes, they're easier than ever to conceal because the delete key removes all traces of an error.

Completing the black and white grids on the computer is as easy as having software, an Internet connection, and time. The most commonly used crossword puzzle software is Across Lite from Literate Software Systems. Most electronic versions from newspapers are distributed in this format, although you'll have to pay for the Internet connection and your crossword puzzle subscription. You can log on to the *New York Times* Web site and download that day's puzzle, or any of the previous puzzles. You can instantly check your answers on the archived puzzles and even chat in the online forum with other solvers when you're done.

The Internet also makes tools easily available to you. There are online tutorials, crossword dictionaries, anagram finders, and everyone's favorite search engines. For the creative minds, there are even crossword compilers to assist you in making your own crossword puzzle.

Who's Out There?

The online availability is fostering a sense of community where
one didn't previously exist. Crossword puzzles are typically a solitary pursuit, unless you happen to be solving with a family member or friend. Previously you could discuss an interesting clue in a
social situation, or perhaps find another colleague who had seen
the puzzle, but that was the extent of it. Nowadays you can hop
on one of many crossword forums and develop a comradery with
others as passionate as you.

I often log on to the *New York Times'* "Today's Puzzle" forum,
just to see what people are saying. The majority of conversations
revolve around clues and solutions from that day's puzzle—or
even tomorrow's puzzle. Many people download the next day's
puzzle when it is available at 10:00 P.M. Eastern Standard Time,
solve it, and discuss it before midnight strikes. When I sign in
and view the posts, I often see congratulations to that day's constructor, as they often frequent the forum, and/or engrossing
critiques of the puzzle's clue meanings and word choices. The
posters rarely mince comments when it comes to dissecting the
puzzles—enjoying the discussion almost as much as the act of
solving the puzzle. Perhaps more. They are very welcoming of
new guests and are quick to integrate them into the dialogue.

Crossword forums aren't always just for the solving enthusiasts. The constructors also share their experiences online in their
own discussion groups—often asking for advice and critiques of
their potential clues in their quest to seeing their puzzles in print.

Nancy Salomon, a crossword constructor from Rochester, New York took up puzzlemaking in 1992. As the online community grew larger, so did her mentoring of new constructors. She told me that as soon as she got online, she was recommended to *www.cruciverb.com*. "That was what opened up everything for me," she said. "I began some private correspondences with other constructors. All of a sudden I was learning a lot in a hurry, not to mention establishing friendships that mean a lot to me. There were so many lessons I learned the hard, solitary way through trial and error. I think that's one of the reasons I really like mentoring. For someone who's hungry to learn, I can dramatically shorten the learning curve."

Nancy believes that the benefit for constructors is enormous, as can be seen below in my discussion with Vic Fleming. "By just checking out the home page, a rookie constructor can get off to a very fast start," she said. "There is helpful advice, specification sheets for various buyers, information about software, and databases and word lists. Newbies are acquiring in a heartbeat what used to take months, if not years."

Nancy went on to say that the two communities (solvers and constructors) tend to steer clear of one another. Some constructors would rather avoid the picky comments and critiques. "For those who have never tried constructing, the set of expectations are often unrealistic," Nancy said. "There are certain vowel-laden words like OREO, ERIE, etc., that are always going to find their way into puzzles. They're the glue that holds the longer, more interesting entries together. Editors and constructors understand this. Not all solvers do."

Finding Virtual Assistance

Vic Fleming, a judge, teacher, and author from Little Rock, Arkansas, learned first hand how effective the crossword community could be in his quest to become a constructor. Vic solves approximately five crossword puzzles a day. On an average morning he solves the *Chicago Tribune* syndicated puzzle in his daily paper at the breakfast table, in ink. During the day, he solves a *Los Angeles Times*, *New York Sun* or CrosSynergy puzzle that he's printed off the Internet, in pencil. At 9:00 P.M. he solves the *New York Times* puzzle as soon as it becomes available online in his state, using the timed applet so the computer can calculate the time it took him to solve the crossword. Lying in bed, later in the evening, he typically solves another puzzle or two that he has printed off of the Internet. On Mondays it takes him less than an hour (combined) to solve all of the puzzles. On Fridays it takes him an approximate two hours to solve them all.

Even I had to wonder why Vic strives to solve all of these puzzles. Why not just stop at one, or three for that matter? "This is an activity I started many years ago—for the challenge, relaxation, and education," he told me. "Since I have become a crossword constructor, it also is now a way of enhancing the work product from my hobby."

In August 2003, Vic took up constructing. "For weeks I jammed and crammed, squeezing letters into hand-drawn grids, self-taught and anxious," he said. "I surfed the Web late at night in search of words, phrases, and definitions. The goal was to quickly master my new hobby and get a puzzle published."

When I ask him how that went, he said, "Moving too fast and taking too much for granted, I generated some impressive rejection notes.. "From Wayne Robert Williams of Tribune Media: 'I am rejecting your puzzle . . . LERNE is unacceptable.' What? LERNE unacceptable? Even though I'm quoting Chaucer? From Will Shortz of the *New York Times*: 'Thanks but regrets on your crossword submission . . . I'm afraid it has a number of problems . . .'"

Then Vic discovered *www.cruciverb.com*—a Web site devoted to puzzle constructors. There he found published constructors engaged in dialogue. Monitoring the exchange of folks who knew what they were doing gave him an education and a new sense of optimism. In late December 2003, he posted his first note to the Cruciverb list, asking a simple question about word lists. "Welcome, Vic," read the first reply. "Have you stumbled across the NYT forum yet?"

This e-mail launched a friendship and mentorship between Vic and two other constructors. They worked with Vic and demonstrated to him their various methodologies. "My first puzzle was accepted in March 2004 and published in late June 2004," he said. "I have now had more than fifty puzzles published; including two in the *New York Times* and twenty in an e-Book (with two other authors) released by Advenio LLC. About three-fourths of these are solo puzzles and one-quarter are in partnership with other constructors I have met in this industry."

Vic continues sharing his passion with others, even teaching a class on crossword puzzles. He discusses the history of crosswords, construction, and even the importance of crosswords in developing a strong vocabulary.

Can't Talk Now, I'm Busy

Nowadays it seems that everyone carries around a cellular phone—whether it's your fourteen-year-old babysitter or your eighty-year-young grandmother. A cell phone allows you to keep in contact, and sometimes fails to give you a way to remain out of touch, with those you love. The phones also provide you with endless sources of entertainment and photo-taking opportunities, depending on which model you have of course. You can even download your favorite crossword puzzles, including the NYT Crossword mobile game. For a mere $3.75 a month, people who own a Verizon Wireless handset can subscribe to the service and download a week's worth of puzzles, and thankfully the corresponding solutions. Nokia and Motorolla phone users can download other games, including The Sun Mobile Crossword game in the United Kingdom.

To try it out, I downloaded the Dell Magazine Crossword demo version onto my Motorola flip phone. I was curious to see what is involved, how small the screen is, and how difficult it would be to type in clues.

After waiting about sixty seconds, the instruction screen appeared. The number 1 clears a letter, 2 through 9 allow me to type letters, and 0 gives me puzzle assistance. When I pushed "Select," the screen disappears and the crossword puzzle is visible. Luckily it only showed me the NW (top left) quadrant of the puzzle and the letters are fairly large. At the bottom of the screen I saw the corresponding Across and Down clue for the square my cursor was currently sitting in. I moved among the squares using the arrow keys at the top of the phone and watched the clues change accordingly. The typing of the letters isn't a horrible task, albeit time consuming, requiring me to push the numeric buttons multiple times to get the correct letter. The grid was a 15 × 15 puzzle, with a fair amount of black squares. I pushed 0 to see what the puzzle assistance provides and found that I can check a letter, a word, or the entire puzzle or show a letter, a word, or the entire puzzle.

My final conclusion was that it's a great device for avoiding conversations and passing time while traveling. But if I have access to the Internet, a newspaper, or crossword puzzle book, I definitely would prefer to solve a crossword in those mediums.

American Crossword Puzzle Tournament

The American Crossword Puzzle Tournament (ACPT) is the nation's oldest and largest crossword competition. Founded in 1978 by Will Shortz, the tournament runs every year in mid-March in Stamford, Connecticut. People from across the United States, and sometimes other countries, compete against each other for cash prizes, trophies, and fame within the crossword community. Since its inception, the tournament has grown to include multiple divisions (age, regional, contestants who have not won in other divisions in previous tournaments, etc.), higher prize amounts, more attendees, and fun events including team puzzles and custom game shows.

When it comes to the tournament itself, the ACPT crossword puzzles are specially commissioned, but the constructors are bound by the same rules in creating tournament puzzles. No puzzle can be based on one particular subject, as it might give some solvers an unfair advantage over the others.

The contestants range from teenagers to the elderly, from a variety of different backgrounds. The event attracts a good amount of teachers, writers, editors, lawyers, and computer programmers, and the male contestants usually outnumber the female ones.

There are seven rounds where the contestants all compete together. The highest three scorers over the seven puzzles participate in the final, where they compete on a stage writing on a board using black erasable markers. They wear headphones that blare white noise to drown out the distractions of audience members and announcers.

Although practicing is the best technique for winning the competition, there are a few ways to gain an advantage. Brushing up on current entertainment, sports, and classical arts is a must. Some even say that you can use strategy when it comes to writing the letters. A lowercase "e" takes less time to write than an upper-case "E", giving competitors an edge on the time, although Ellen Ripstein, a freelancer from New York City, is quick to disagree that there's any advantage in that. "Lowercase letters, special Es, etc. are just a myth, at least among the top solvers. These handwriting 'tricks' succeed only in annoying the judges." Ellen has participated in almost every year's tournament since its onset in 1978. The only year she missed was 1979. Growing up, she came from a family of puzzle fanatics. Her parents bought an extra copy of the Sunday edition of the *New York Times* just for the crossword, and they were the neighborhood authorities on puzzles. "As soon as I could write, I happily filled in children's puzzles tucked into drawings of bunny rabbits and kangaroos, with words like CAT crossed with the A in BEAR," Ellen said. "Progressing through Dell easy, medium, and hard puzzles, I was soon completing the Simon & Schuster crossword books my parents left in the bathroom. Crosswords were a part of life. I never dreamed that this solitary pastime could be tested in competition, and that I would turn out to be one of the best solvers in the country."

In early 1978, Ellen was solving the *New York Times* puzzle one day, when she noticed a small advertisement inviting crossword buffs to the first American Crossword Puzzle Tournament in Stamford, Connecticut. "It hasn't been done before," said the flyer, "so who is better than you?" Why not, she thought.

"So on a Saturday morning in March I found myself in a hotel ballroom with 164 other brave souls, including a college friend I dragged along for moral support," Ellen recounted. "The room was reminiscent of the SATs, with long partitioned tables, a large clock, proctors in striped shirts, and deathly silence. Original puzzles had been commissioned for the event, and we were the guinea pigs."

When the dust had settled, Ellen found that she had finished in thirty-first place. "Since I left large pieces blank in at least one puzzle, I was pleased with my standing." After that first Stamford tournament, Ellen saw crossword tournaments go through an upsurge, something that hadn't occurred in the United Sates since the 1920s. *Games* magazine held U.S. Open tournaments from 1982 to 1986. Ellen traveled to these whenever she could, consistently competing well, and she often reached the finals. She won in the New Jersey competitions in 1986 and 1987. "As my results improved, tournaments ceased to be a lark and became serious business. I was now expected to perform well and felt tremendous pressure."

The ACPT continued to be a sore spot for Ellen. "I was almost always in the top five, and had reached the final three twelve times—but by 2001 still had not won," Ellen said. "The closest I came was in 1988. I finished the playoff puzzle first, only to find that I had made a careless error and written SENSELESeNESS instead of SENSELESsNESS. It crossed the extremely obscure word TEMSE which I had as TEMEE. In the finals, accuracy trumps all; a perfect puzzle wins over an imperfect one finished earlier, so I was out of luck."

According to Ellen, her string of near-wins led to the nickname "the Susan Lucci of crosswords," paralleling the soap star's
nineteen nominations before winning an Emmy.

I ask Ellen how it felt to finally win the tournament in 2001.
"It's easy to say in hindsight, but 2001 was charmed," she said.
"The planets were specially aligned. Earlier that year, a contestant
told his friend at the *Wall Street Journal* about me, which led to
a front-page article, complete with sketch, appearing a few days
before the tournament. This in turn led to major media coverage
at the event. Reporters and cameras covered my every move, and
they couldn't have had a better script."

After the first seven puzzles, Ellen's usual rivals for the finals
had all finished just short of the top five. Instead, she found herself competing against Al Sanders and Patrick Jordan. Ellen tells
me about that final puzzle. "As the playoff proceeded, I oblivi-
ously solved the puzzle," she said, "only hoping not to panic and
leave half of it blank. This didn't happen, and I was working
as usual, not knowing how anyone else was doing. Although
headphones blocked out the running commentary, I could still
sense rustles in the room and there was a big one at one point,
and I knew someone else had finished. It turned out Patrick Jordan was done—but "with a mistake!" breathed the commentator,
though I didn't know it at the time. He had written PAST instead
of MAST, his own version of SENSELESENESS."

Before the tournament, Will Shortz had been quoted as saying the crowd would "blow the roof off the hotel" if Ellen won.
In response, the Marriott left a fruit basket and welcome letter

in her room. "Best of luck this weekend," it said. "We will have the roofers stand by." Ellen finished the puzzle and removed her headphones to a massive roar. "Are you sure? Are you sure?" she asked the judges and burst into tears. Behind her, a contestant unfurled a sign saying "Rrrrripstein. This is the year!" He had been bringing it for years and finally got to use it (she has it now). She has a homemade video of the finals, as well as tapes of the television coverage. "To this day, when I see the footage, I burst into tears," she said. "I'm in tears right now, just writing about it. The emotional release was not to be matched. I won. I finally, finally won."

Ellen hasn't won the tournament since 2001. She said that the win took enormous drive and energy. "Now I'm older and slower," she said. "The eyes get strained, the hand gets tired, and young whippersnappers are ready to pounce." Her standings post-win have been tenth, fifth, fifteenth, and eleventh. She's considered retiring, but said it would be nice to make the top five again.

When I asked Ellen how she prepares for the tournaments, she said that you have to solve crossword puzzles every day, lots and lots of them. "It's good, old-fashioned practice. Near a tournament, I'll whip through ten, twenty-five, even fifty puzzles a day." She said that the constant solving gets you used to physically writing and inures you to any crosswordese terms. She also has tips for during a tournament. She said, "Don't do just the acrosses or downs—read every clue and be careful not to miswrite letters. Don't try to fill in long entries, but work on the shorter ones until you can determine the theme. If totally stuck on a square, go through the alphabet. And use the remainder of the minute to double-check your paper."

The American Crossword Puzzle Tournaments are each March. Of course, if you can't make it, you can always play along at home. You can register along with everyone else and receive a full set of the 2005 tournament puzzles. After solving them, you send back your solutions and your times. Your submissions are judged, and you'll receive your unofficial scores and ranking in the various divisions you were eligible to compete.

And the Youngest Winner (Thus Far) Is . . .

Tyler Hinman is the youngest crossword enthusiast to win the ACPT, which he did in 2005 when he was twenty years old. This was not his only time participating in the tournament. He first entered in 2001, when he was sixteen, after he had only been solving crosswords for a couple of years. "I've been doing puzzles in general forever, but it was in ninth grade that I got into crosswords," he said. "My history teacher gave me one during a boring Friday study hall . . . it happened to be that day's *New York Times* puzzle, so I didn't do too well on it. I was still hooked, and clipped the puzzle out every day from the *International Herald-Tribune* (my family was living in England at the time). I've been doing them ever since in ever-increasing quantities." According to Tyler's personal Web site, he wrote in only one of those answers on that first puzzle, and that entry was incorrect.

In the 2001 competition, Tyler placed 101st. He missed attending the following year, but took the challenge at home and according to their results, he would have placed number sixty-four. He was able to go to the tournament in 2003 where he placed twentieth, and again in 2004 where he moved up seven notches to thirteenth place.

I asked Tyler what made him enter the competition. "I'm really not sure," he pondered. "I guess it was any combination of my natural competitiveness, my desire to see just how good I'd gotten at these things, and my curiosity about what sounded like a fun weekend of puzzling with other word nerds. It was fun (despite coming over from England for my first tournament, resulting in about four hours of sleep over the whole weekend), and I kept coming back."

I wondered if Tyler uses anything to prepare for the competition. "Nothing special," he said. "I solve obscene amounts of puzzles year-round, so I just stuck with that. Well, I guess I did buy a book of easyish Sunday puzzles (a Maura Jacobson collection) to time myself."

I went on to ask Tyler about the competition itself. "It's an interesting scene outside of the competition," he answered. "You've got people sitting in the lobby and banquet hall playing board games and doing puzzles, like the Marriott is their living room. Inside, you see upward of five hundred people seated in rows, all gearing up nervously for the next puzzle." He was happy to meet Will Shortz, considering that he admires Will and his puzzles, and he was glad to become acquainted with the

other attendees as well. "Either they were renowned constructors that I was honored to meet, or fellow solvers that became
friends."

I was curious to know how Tyler feels after winning the tournament, although I was sure I could guess some of the feelings.
"Amazing. Flabbergasting. Surreal. Pick one. I didn't know what
to do, how to carry myself. It didn't even feel real." Right up until
Will Shortz announced him as the winner, there was still part of
Tyler that was saying, "Something has to go wrong here at some
point; I couldn't have just won this thing."

Did Tyler think he could win the entire competition? Of
course. "I knew I could do it, but I was surprised it came together
so quickly," he relates. "My ranking rose significantly every year,
and every year I could feel my skills improving. Nonetheless,
they say there's a ceiling after you make it to the top level of
competition, a barrier that's tough to break through. Add in my
age disadvantage (they don't just take trivia from the 90s and 00s,
you know), and it's pretty amazing that I took the title two years
after entering the A division. But, at the same time, I knew I had
done what it takes to get to be the champion."

Tyler said he will definitely be returning next year to defend
his title, although he said it's difficult for anyone to repeat. He does
want to prove that he can win again, since his victory included a
dose of luck. During the final round, Al Sanders, a veteran finalist
at the tournament, was ahead of Tyler and the other competitor
when he made a huge error. Sanders signaled that he was done,
when in fact he had left two squares empty. Tyler finished more

than three minutes later than Al, but he completed the grid and won the tournament.

I asked Tyler if he had any parting advice and crossword tips. "Read and write at the same time. The skill will be your best friend." He also suggests practicing as much as you can. "I didn't study dictionaries or encyclopedias to become skilled. I just solved a metric ton of puzzles." Unlike Ellen, Tyler told me that it can help to write your letters efficiently. "In 2005, I switched from the three-lined I (the vertical line and two crossbars) to the one-lined I. And I won the tournament. Coincidence? Well, yeah, probably, but it can shave off a few seconds. Next year I'm thinking of writing my E's like the Greek letter sigma." His last suggestion is to keep a spare yellow #2 pencil handy. A jammed mechanical pencil can bring down the best.

Competitive Nature

So is there a way for crossword enthusiasts to compete in a tournament and still use the Zen philosophy? Of course. Warrior Zen, or Samurai Zen, was adopted by the samurai when they came into power several hundred years ago in Japan. They brought Zen into the arena of warfare, maneuvering the Zen concepts of calmness and being centered onto the battlefield. Their quest was to be fully present in combat, regardless of the stakes. They strove to become detached from the warfare and to train their minds to react as if their activity was as indifferent as plowing a field. Suzoki Shosan, a Zen Warrior, wrote, "The warrior meditates only when he is performing his duty. As soon as he puts aside his sword, he relaxes his attention." Their moves and attitude became automatic, allowing them to compete and conquer as needed.

In the ACPT, or any other crossword competition, you're not out to slaughter your opponent, but there are ways to work toward succeeding into those coveted final three spots. Along with the skills and tips discussed, you can practice to make your solving techniques automatic. You can work to center yourself and ignore the abnormal hubbub surrounding the competition that can easily distract you from the task at hand. You can dissolve your ego and resolve to compete without any fear of mistakes or embarrassment. And you very well may win the tournament.

Sudoku

Sudoku means "single number" in Japanese and is a crossword-like puzzle that is sweeping the globe. Also known as "Number Place" in the United States, Sudoku uses a square grid that measures nine squares by nine squares. Instead of clues, the grid contains an amount of "given" digits within the eighty-one squares—each given being a value from one and nine. The number of these digits that are initially provided, along with the placement of those digits, determines the level of difficulty of the specific puzzle. Obviously the more givens, the easier the puzzle is intended to be.

There is one rule and instruction to the puzzle of Sudoku. Each column, each row, and each of the internal nine three by three grids must contain the numerals one through nine once and only once. Each puzzle has only one correct solution. The game is not mathematical in nature; in fact the numbers are used for convenience only. You could replace the digits with letters, shapes, or any other representation and still have the same game. The concept of the puzzle is simple to understand, which is perhaps why there are a large number of people willing to give it a spin. As they go along, these same people learn that they must use logic skills to get anywhere in solving the puzzle.

The history of Sudoku stems back to the 1700s and Swiss mathematician Leonhard Euler. He first presented the puzzle in 1783 as Euler's "Latin Squares." The only difference between his creation and the present day grid is that the puzzle was not subdivided into the nine three by three squares. Instead solvers just needed to place the numbers one through nine into each row and column without any overlap.

Almost two hundred years later, the puzzle was reinvented and printed in the magazine *Math Puzzles and Logic Problems*, published by Dell with the name "Number Place." The puzzle was later produced as "Suuji wa dokushin ni kagiru" (meaning that number is limited only single) in *Monthly Nikolist* in 1984 by the company Nikoli in Japan. That name was shortened to Sudoku and in 1986 Nikoli provided further innovations by restricting the number of givens to a maximum of thirty, and requiring puzzles to be symmetrical in the positioning of the givens. In 1997 Wayne Gould, a retired Hong Kong judge, found a Sudoku puzzle in a bookstore and decided to invent a software program that would create puzzles at random. Six years later he had a finished product that he proceeded to market to a variety of publications. The

Times in Britain scooped up the puzzle and many other newspapers followed suit. Today Sudoku puzzles can be found in magazines and newspapers across the globe.

After reading up on the rules, I decide to sit down to tackle my first Sudoku puzzle, an easy one. I begin by plugging in some numbers, and easily complete a few of the rows and columns with no duplicate digits. I happily work through the puzzle, assuming it must be beginner's luck, as I'm not even really using a system to place the numbers. That smile quickly fades as I realize that I'm almost finished, but I can't place two numbers in the grid to complete two rows because they already exist in one of the three by three regions. And that's when I figure out one of the major differences between Sudoku and a regular crossword puzzle: the mistakes.

When you make a mistake in a crossword puzzle, you can easily look back to that one clue and fix it. You might have to make a few adjustments to some of the surrounding answers, but for the most part, your error is self-contained and correctable. In Sudoku, there is really no way to work backward and just rotate a couple of numbers. Believe me, I try! I switch two numbers around, which causes me to flip a couple more, and then I find myself at a halt, with nowhere else to go.

I decide to wipe the grid clean (a common occurrence I find) and try to employ a technique or two. I start scanning through the areas with a large amount of givens, quickly realizing that the number eight can only go in one location in a particular column. This allows me to place a few more numbers, and I'm quickly moving forward. When I am no longer able to analyze the grid, I make a couple of guesses (keeping my fingers crossed) and complete the puzzle—all in less than ten minutes. What a relief.

I decide to research the puzzle further and determine if there are other techniques to employ. I find that when faced with a decision between multiple digits for a square, some solvers choose to pencil in those possible numbers in small print in the corner of the squares. They then move forward and hope that they can later return to place the candidates in their correct positions. Others employ a dot method where they place a pattern of dots in the corners of the square depending on the digit(s) they are considering.

Sudoku definitely employs a different part of your brain when compared to crossword puzzles. Sudoku puzzles are based on logic, while crosswords are solved with language and cultural knowledge. Together, the two make for a rather compatible duo when it comes to working your brain and getting your puzzle fix.

I Don't Want To!

Although the crossword puzzle continues to evolve and change, being released in new formats and spin-off puzzles, there are those crossword fans that resist anything but a traditional paper grid. Perhaps they are new to computers, or are perfectly comfortable with their current crossword skills, but they're not growing and adapting with the industry.

Zen is about adaptation, not defeat. As the rules change, it's important that you work to accept them and learn them to the best of your ability. When you make a mistake or don't complete a puzzle, you need to learn from the process. When you try out a new type of crossword, attempt to solve them with a friend, or move out of your normal (secure) boundaries, you should attempt to adapt to the circumstance.

Being resistant to the current state of anything, even crossword puzzles, is equivalent to paddling against the current. You're going to get nowhere, and you just might drown. Those who ignore the benefits and availability of mobile puzzles may find themselves soon without any source of enjoyment. Who knows what the future may bring, and what mediums puzzles may evolve into.

In Zen you work toward the ultimate goal of detachment from the objects and notions surrounding you, which means that attachment to these things is the source of suffering. By someone staying attached to her current crossword books and solving techniques, she's creating unnecessary stress when she thinks about the "newfangled" puzzles that others enjoy. It's best to go with the flow and at the very least accept the current state of technology. The same goes for a business that wants to place their products online or a new invention that works only with mobile devices.

Going with the flow doesn't necessarily mean that you go undirected and free. You don't have to bounce around from place to place, idea to idea, new technology to new technology. It means that you find a line of movement and go with it, rather than fight against it.

The following koan serves to illustrate this very thought:

The Zen master Hakuin was praised by his neighbors as one living a pure life.

A beautiful Japanese girl whose parents owned a food store lived near him. Suddenly, without any warning, her parents discovered she was with child.

This made her parents angry. She would not confess who the man was, but after much harassment at last named Hakuin.

In great anger the parent went to the master. "Is that so?" was all he would say.

After the child was born it was brought to Hakuin. By this time he had lost his reputation, which did not trouble him, but he took very good care of the child. He obtained milk from his neighbors and everything else he needed.

A year later the girl-mother could stand it no longer. She told her parents the truth—the real father of the child was a young man who worked in the fishmarket.

The mother and father of the girl at once went to Hakuin to ask forgiveness, to apologize at length, and to get the child back.

Hakuin was willing. In yielding the child, all he said was: "Is that so?"

Hakuin knew that the child was not his, but he went with the direction of the situation. Had he rebelled and pushed back, the event would have escalated with blame, hatred, and accusations. After raising the child for a year, he was also willing to relinquish all ties, again continuing to go with the flow of the circumstances.

Try This

If you haven't already, solve a crossword puzzle online. You can find Web sites that will offer you free crosswords, or trial puzzles, before you commit to any subscriptions. Revel in the process and learning the new software, maybe even cheat and reveal a letter or a solution just to see how it works. If you currently solve puzzles on your computer, try using a timed applet and see how your skills work against the clock. Don't do it with your ego's intentions where you try to beat other solver's times. Instead use the competitive nature to master yourself and increase your individual speed and accuracy.

On the Move

1 Computer rodent
6 Navity scene representation
12 Fluttering tree
13 Discarded
14 Delayed recording
15 Soda measurement
16 To supplement with great effort (with out)
17 Glided through the water
19 Shade tree
22 Variable rate mortgage
24 Ball
25 Solo vocal
26 Black color
28 Descendant
29 Handheld communication device
33 First horoscope sign
34 Turkey sandwich condiment

35 Intense feeling
36 ___ & Jerry's ice cream
37 Have
40 London stock exchange (abbr.)
41 Not out of
43 Snack
45 Dilbert creator ___ Adams
48 Clear liquor
50 Maryland baseball team
52 Gardening tool
53 Champion
54 Desires

1 Team partner
2 Japanese city
3 Higher
4 Visit
5 Tails
6 Small morsel
7 Carried out
8 Top left keyboard button
9 Single oat cereal
10 Him
11 Education (abbr.)

13 Organized competitions
18 Sheared fiber
20 MGM's logo
21 Neck hair
23 Small diamond
25 Sneezy's sound
27 Public transportation
28 Snoop
29 Telephone
30 Greek god of love
31 Resides (2 words)
32 Scold
36 Chomper
38 Triangular object
39 Bare
42 Kitchen appliance
44 Sticky substances
46 Against
47 Bullfight shout
49 Lyric poem
50 Ouch!
51 Providence state

Appendix A

Crossword Resources

This section is devoted to providing you sources and Web sites for furthering your crossword experiences and skills.

Online Crossword Puzzles

Guardian Unlimited—Cryptic
✍*www.guardianunlimited.co.uk/crossword*

The Globe and Mail—Cryptic
✍*www.globeandmail.com/crosswords*

Houston Chronicle
✍*www.chron.com/content/fun/games/xword/index.html*

London Times—Cryptic
✍*www.timesonline.co.uk/section/0,,252,00.html*

The New York Times
✍*www.nytimes.com/pages/crosswords/index.html*

Newsday
✍*www.newsday.com/features/puzzles/ny-puzzle-crossword-htmlstory,0,4692820.htmlstory*

Sudoku
www.sudoku.com

Sydney Morning Herald
www.crossword.smh.com.au

USA Today
www.puzzles.usatoday.com

Washington Post Sunday Puzzle
*www.washingtonpost.com/wp-srv/style/crosswords/daily/
    front.htm*

Crossword Helpers

a2z Word Finder
A free online dictionary for crosswords, Scrabble dictionary,
    Literati helper, Jumble solver, WordOx helper, anagram
    generator, and vocabulary utility.
www.a2zwordfinder.com

Allwords.com
Search for definitions in a variety of languages using full or
    partial words.
www.allwords.com

Anagram Genius
Very powerful anagram creator.
www.anagramgenius.com

Cliché Finder

Over 3,300 indexed clichés to search.

✍*www.westegg.com/cliche*

Crossword Cracker

Software to search for crossword clues, anagrams, and
   Scrabble searches.

✍*www.crosswordweaver.com*

Crossword Helper

Word database to help you find the missing letters you're in
   search of.

✍*www.casr.adelaide.edu.au/craig/wow.html*

Dictionary.com

Online dictionary and thesaurus.

✍*www.dictionary.com*

Merriam-Webster OnLine

Search the online dictionary, thesaurus, and Encyclopedia
   Britannica.

✍*www.m-w.com*

More Words

Enter in patterns and missing letters to find crossword solutions and Scrabble words.

✍*www.morewords.com*

OneAcross

Enter in clues and/or patterns to find possible crossword
  solutions.

www.oneacross.com

RhymeZone

Enter in a word and find its rhymes, synonyms, definitions,
  uses in literature, and more.

www.rhymezone.com

TEA Crossword Helper

Downloadable software comes with its own database to
  search while offline.

www.bryson.ltd.uk/tea.html

Crossword Software

Across Lite

Free, required software to solve many of the online crossword puzzles.

www.litsoft.com

Crossword Compiler

Construction software with an online clue database, grid
  database, and much more.

www.crossword-compiler.com

Crossword Construction Kit

This software assists you in construction crossword puzzles
  using templates and pre-existing words, or you are free to
  incorporate your own designs and solutions.
www.crosswordkit.com

Crossword Maestro

Software that greatly assists in explaining and solving cryptic crosswords.
www.crosswordmaestro.com

Crossword Weaver

Crossword puzzle–making software with many preloaded
  options, including cryptic grids.
www.crosswordweaver.com

CrossWorks

Crossword construction software that comes complete with
  the Merriam-Webster dictionary database. They even rec-
  ommend copying your newspaper layout into their inter-
  face for faster and easier solving.
www.homeware.com

Shockwave Plug-in

Free downloadable software to solve crossword puzzles
  using the Macromedia plug-in on your computer.
www.macromedia.com/software/shockwaveplayer/

Online Puzzle Makers

Crossword Puzzle Games
Enter up to twenty words and clues, and the software creates the puzzle online.
✍*www.crosswordpuzzlegames.com/create.html*

Variety Games
Enter the title, words, and clues online and the software creates the puzzle for you to save.
✍*www.varietygames.com/cw*

Fun with Crossword Puzzles

A Personalized Crossword Puzzle
Send as much personal information as you can and obtain a personalized puzzle—great for gifts!
✍*www.macnamarasband.com/personalized.html*

American Crossword Puzzle Tournament
Information, news, recaps, and next year's sign up information for the American Crossword Puzzle Tournament
✍*www.crosswordtournament.com*

Crossword Greeting Cards
Animated online greeting cards to send to friends and family.
www.123greetings.com/events/crossword_puzzle_day/

Puzzle Prezzents

Find crossword-themed gifts for clients and friends.

✎*www.puzzleprezzents.com*

Education

About Puzzles

Links, reviews, and information on American crossword
puzzles, cryptic puzzles, and many other games.

✎*www.puzzles.about.com*

Yet Another Guide to Cryptic Crosswords

A wealth of information on the types of cryptic clues, solving tips, and puzzle sources.

✎*www.biddlecombe.demon.co.uk/yagcc/index.html*

Crossword Puzzle Solutions

**Much Ado about
Crosswords**

Piecing It Together

Scratch That One

Twister

Stress-Free

S.O.S.

A Blank Slate

The Art of Manipulation

The Many Benefits

On the Move

Index

Printed in the United States
By Bookmasters